Crazy Games

ULTIMATE travel GAMES

D1405208

PRICE STERN SLOAN
Published by the Penguin Group

Penguin Group (USA) Inc., 375 Hudson Street, New York, New York 10014, U.S.A.
Penguin Group (Canada), 90 Eglinton Avenue East, Suite 700, Toronto, Ontario,
Canada M4P 2Y3 (a division of Pearson Penguin Canada Inc.)
Penguin Books Ltd, 80 Strand, London WC2R 0RL, England
Penguin Ireland, 25 St Stephen's Green, Dublin 2, Ireland
(a division of Penguin Books Ltd)
Penguin Group (Australia), 250 Camberwell Road, Camberwell, Victoria 3124, Australia
(a division of Pearson Australia Group Pty Ltd)
Penguin Books India Pvt Ltd, 11 Community Centre, Panchsheel Park,
New Delhi - 110 017, India
Penguin Group (NZ), Cnr Airborne and Rosedale Roads, Albany, Auckland 1310,
New Zealand (a division of Pearson New Zealand Ltd)
Penguin Books (South Africa) (Pty) Ltd, 24 Sturdee Avenue, Rosebank,
Johannesburg 2196, South Africa

Penguin Books Ltd, Registered Offices:
80 Strand, London WC2R 0RL, England

The scanning, uploading, and distribution of this book via the Internet or via any
other means without the permission of the publisher is illegal and punishable by law.
Please purchase only authorized electronic editions, and do not participate in or
encourage electronic piracy of copyrighted materials. Your support of the author's
rights is appreciated.

Designed by Debbie Guy-Christiansen. Cover illustration by Matthew Applebaum.
Peace-sign illustration page 40 based on art © Joel Jansson, Sweden.

© 2006 by Price Stern Sloan. All rights reserved. Published by Price Stern Sloan,
a division of Penguin Young Readers Group, 345 Hudson Street, New York,
New York 10014. PSS! is a registered trademark of Penguin Group (USA) Inc.
Manufactured in China.

10 9 8 7 6 5 4 3 2 1

ISBN 0-8431-2007-X

Crazy Games

ULTIMATE
travel
GAMES

Written by
Micol Ostow

PSSI
PRICE STERN SLOAN

contents

"Are we there yet?"

C hances are, at *some* point during *some* trip with your parents, you've asked that question. Probably more than once. But who can blame you? Traveling—long lists of items to pack, stop-and-go traffic, waiting in line at train stations or airports—can be totally tedious. So what's a kid to do? Well, why not take matters into your own hands? In *Crazy Games: Ultimate Travel Games* you'll find hours of on-the-go entertainment—right at your fingertips!

With board games, riddles, tongue twisters, word games, and more, *Ultimate Travel Games* is packed full of everything you need to keep busy, bust boredom, and generally have a blast. What are you waiting for?

TRAVEL BINGO

Look around for the travel-related items pictured on the two boards here, then cover those items with a checker as you see them.

To play by yourself:
Time yourself—see how long it takes you to cover an entire board.

To play with two people:
The first person to cover an entire row—horizontally, vertically, or diagonally—wins!

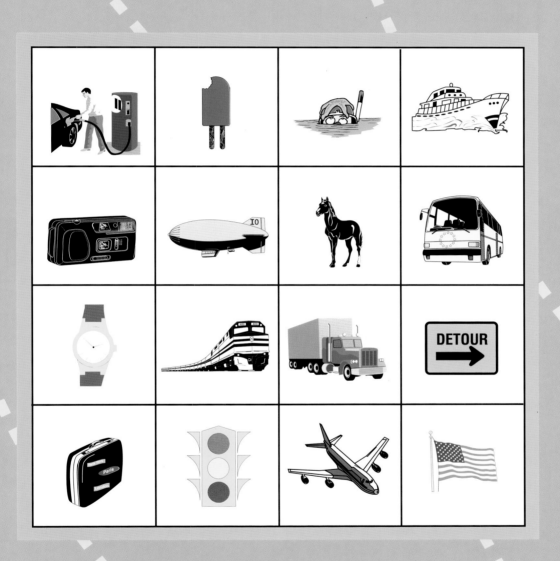

MANCALA

Mancala may just be the oldest game still played today! The word "mancala" is believed to be Arabic, and its English translation is "to transfer." The object of the game is to transfer your playing pieces from one bin to another. In our version, you'll use suitcases as bins.

> **Did you KNOW?** Variations on mancala are played in India, Sri Lanka, Egypt, Indonesia, North America, Malaysia, the Caribbean, Europe, the Philippines, along the east coast of South America, and throughout Africa.

HOW TO PLAY

Each player grabs any eighteen checkers (color doesn't matter) and places three checkers in each of the six bins closest to him or her. The two larger bins (called the kalahas) on the end of the board are left empty.

Once you've decided who will go first, that player then scoops up all the pieces from any bin on his or her side of the board. Moving to the right, that player drops one piece in each bin as he or she goes along the board. If you come to your large bin, your kalaha, drop a piece in there, too. If, after you put a piece in the kalaha, you still have pieces in your hand, continue to put pieces in the bins on your opponent's side. If you should reach the other end where your opponent's kalaha is, skip over it and continue on your side. If your last piece falls in your kalaha, you get to take another turn. If not, then it is your opponent's turn. He or she does the same.

When the last piece that you drop is in an "empty" bin, you get to capture the opponent's playing pieces in the bin directly next to your bin. These pieces are then put into your kalaha along with the piece that was in the empty bin. After the capture, it is the other player's turn.

The object of the game is to be the player with the most pieces in your kalaha. When all six bins on your side or the other player's side are empty, the game is over. The player who still has pieces in his or her bins can now put them in the kalaha. Each player counts his or her pieces, and the one with the most pieces is the winner!

CHINESE CHECKERS

Game Setup

Chinese checkers is easy to learn and can be played by almost anybody, of any age, at any time. This makes it the perfect game for family vacations!

First, each player must choose a game piece color. Next, each player puts six game pieces of the chosen color on the six marks in the nearest of the star's points.

Rules

Each player can make one move per turn. Moves must follow the direction of the lines on the board. Players can jump over one of their own or one of their opponents' game pieces—without removing the pieces that have been jumped over—but may only jump into an empty game space. Successive jumps are considered legal as long as there are successive empty spaces on the board.

Note that a player is *not* permitted to refuse to move out of his or her starting point in order to prevent an opponent from winning the game.

Object

The first person to get all of his or her game pieces into the opposite point of the star is the winner of the game.

Did you Know? Chinese checkers is neither from China, nor is it a version of checkers. In fact, the game was first released in Germany in 1892!

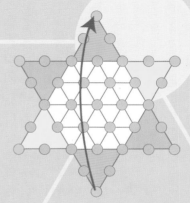

```
Y A W H G I H R T B U S V L
P T V T S R O A D T R I P I
X I W L M A T S I R U O T C
A C T W E F E P F P L E O E
U K N S F O L Q G R Y M A N
N E A X T O N D Q E T E J S
O T I C K O R I R Q I L K E
I C R F E R P E J S C E J P
T B P L A Z H T I O I V H L
A Y L Y W T A X I G Z A V A
C D A B E R Y H H J N R K T
A C N W E A I R P O R T M E
V A E S U I T C A S E F G N
T R I P F N I L D F B U S P
A C G R E S T A U R A N T U
```

For answers, see page 48.

15

BACKGAMMON

Backgammon is a game of luck and skill. It is played by two people with fifteen game pieces each on a board consisting of twenty-four spaces or **points.** You can use your checkers. The checkers are moved according to rolls of the dice. Each player tries to bring his or her own checkers home and "bear them off" before his opponent does, hitting and blocking the enemy checkers along the way.

Did you KNOW? Backgammon has been around a very long time, with origins dating back possibly five thousand years. The ancient Greeks played. So did the Romans. The game we know today was refined in England in the seventeenth century, which is also when it acquired the name "backgammon."

BOARD SETUP

Backgammon is a game for two players, played on a board consisting of twenty-four narrow triangles called **points**. The triangles alternate in color and are grouped into four quadrants of six triangles each. The quadrants are referred to as a player's **home board** and **outer board**, and the opponent's home board and outer board. The home and outer boards are separated from each other by a ridge down the center of the board called the **bar**.

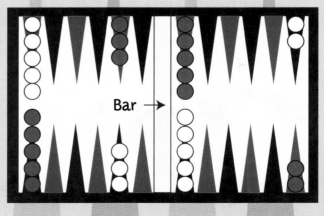

Outer Board   Red's Home Board

Bar →

Outer Board   White's Home Board

The points are numbered for either player starting in that player's home board. The outermost point is the twenty-four point, which is also the opponent's one point. Each player has fifteen checkers of his or her own color. The initial arrangement of checkers is: two on each player's twenty-four point, five on each player's thirteen point, three on each player's eight point, and five on each player's six point.

OBJECT OF THE GAME

The object of the game is for a player to move all of his checkers, or men, into his own home board and then bear them off. The first player to bear off all of his checkers wins the game.

BASIC PLAY

Play proceeds in opposite directions. Each player casts one die, and the player who rolls a higher number moves first, using the two numbers rolled to determine the order of play. If both players roll the same number, each rolls again.

Each player's turn begins with the roll of two dice. The player then moves one or more men in accordance with the numbers cast. For instance, if a 4 and 2 are rolled, the player could move one man four points and another man two points, or move one man four points and then move the same man two more points, or vice-versa. If the player elects to move the same man twice in a turn, that player must land on both the points indicated by the dice. He or she may not simply move the total number of points (in this case, six) if the man cannot advance in the increments (in this case, two and four) indicated by the dice.

The player can only land on a point if the opponent does not own the point (see "Making Points" on the next page). If the opponent does own the point, the player must move a different man. If the player cannot move any men because the opponent owns all the possible points that the player has rolled, the player forfeits the turn. Players alternate turns.

A player who rolls doubles plays the numbers shown on the dice twice. A roll of 6 and 6 means that the player has four sixes to use, and he may move any combination of checkers he feels appropriate to complete this requirement.

A player must use both numbers of a roll if this is legally possible (or all four numbers of a double). When only one number can be played, the player must play that number. Or if either number can be played but not both, the player must play the larger one. When neither number can be used, the player loses his turn. In the case of doubles, when all four numbers cannot be played, the player must play as many numbers as he can.

MAKING POINTS

A player makes a **point** by positioning two or more of his men on it. He then owns that point, and his opponent can neither own that point nor touch down on it when taking a turn until the owner moves all or all but one of his checkers from that point.

PRIME

A player who has made six consecutive points has completed a **prime**. Any opponent trapped behind a prime cannot move past it, since even if the opponent chooses to use the same man twice, that piece must land on the point indicated by each die and would have to touch down on one of those occupied points.

HITTING AND ENTERING

A point occupied by a single checker of either color is called a **blot.** If an opposing checker lands on a blot, the blot is **hit** and placed on the **bar.**

Anytime a player has one or more checkers on the bar, he first must **enter** those checkers into the opposing home board. A checker is entered by moving it to an open point corresponding to one of the numbers on the rolled dice.

LICENSE PLATES ACROSS THE STATES

Check off the states on the U.S. map below as you drive past cars with corresponding license plates!

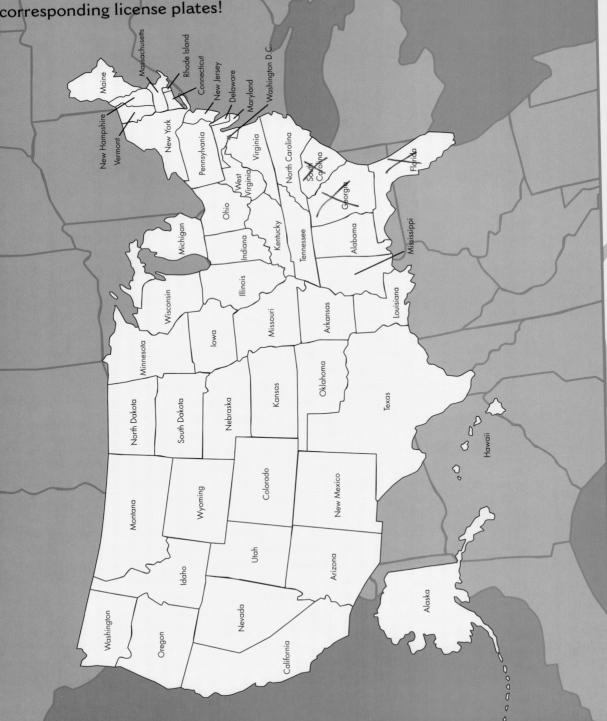

CHECKERS

Game Setup

Checkers is a two-player game. One person picks twelve black pieces, and one person picks twelve white pieces. Set your pieces up on the game board like this:

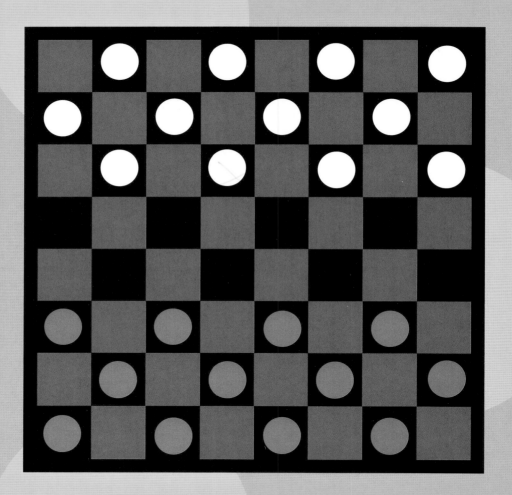

Rules

Players take turns, moving one checker per turn. A checker moves diagonally forward to an empty black square, one square at a time (except for kings—but we'll get to that in a moment).

JUMPING

A player captures an opponent's checker by jumping over it when the square behind the opponent's checker is empty. A checker can make multiple jumps as long as the jumps are moving forward. A player *must* jump whenever possible. Note that when a player jumps over his or her opponent's checker, that checker is captured by the player. The first player to either capture all of his or her opponent's checkers or to block his opponent from moving any remaining checkers is the winner of the game.

CROWNING

When a checker reaches the first row of his or her opponent's side of the board, it becomes a king. A king can move the same way that a plain checker moves, but it can also move backward. Moves in both directions can be combined in a series of jumps.

Did you KNOW? Versions of checkers have been played dating back to the time of the pharaohs in Egypt!

CHESS

Chess is a slightly more complicated game than checkers, and requires just a little more strategy if you're in it to win. But just so that you can keep it in mind, the king is your most important game piece. The goal of the game is to capture your opponent's king before your opponent captures yours. Your king is all that matters. Long live the "king"!

GAME SETUP

Each player has six different types of chess pieces: There are eight pawns, two rooks, two knights, two bishops, one queen, and one king. The pawns are the smallest pieces. The rooks look like tiny little castles with jagged edges along the top. The knights look like little horse heads. The bishops have rounded tops. The king is the tallest piece and has a cross on top. The last piece is the queen, which is the second tallest piece and has a little crown around the top.

Here's a picture:

Pawn   Knight   Bishop   Rook   Queen   King

Each player picks a color and sets up his or her board just like here:

MOE (black)

	A	B	C	D	E	F	G	H
8	ROOK	KNIGHT	BISHOP	QUEEN	KING	BISHOP	KNIGHT	ROOK
7	pawn	pawn	pawn	pawn	pawn	pawn	pawn	pawn
6								
5								
4								
3								
2	pawn	pawn	pawn	pawn	pawn	pawn	pawn	pawn
1	ROOK	KNIGHT	BISHOP	QUEEN	KING	BISHOP	KNIGHT	ROOK

YOU (white)

Note that the rows and columns of a chess board are actually called the ranks and files. Each rank and file has its own corresponding letter and number.

Moving The Pieces Around The Board

Every piece has different rules about how it can move. But first, keep in mind that only one piece can ever be in a square at a time. So if you want to put your piece in a square that already has a piece in it, you have two options:

1. If the piece in the square is yours, you have to move it out of the way before you can occupy it.
2. If the piece in the square is your opponent's, then you can "capture" this piece. You then put your piece in the box on the board, and take the opponent's piece off the board. That piece is now out of play forever. You cannot continue to move your piece once you have captured something.

The Rook

The rook is very easy: It moves only up and down, or side to side. It can't go diagonal or sideways or anything else except along a rank or a file. It is not allowed to jump over any pieces. The chessboard here shows how a rook is allowed to move. This shows ONE move. If you want to move the rook from C4 to E6, you'd have to first move the rook from C4 to E4, and then on your next turn from E4 to E6. This goes for all pieces: Whatever the piece's rule, it lasts one turn.

The Bishop

The bishop can move only in a diagonal line for as many spaces as it likes until something blocks it. It also cannot jump over any other pieces during its move. Since bishops only move in diagonal lines, they'll always stay on the same color square that they started on (one starts on a black square, and one on a white). The chessboard here shows how a bishop can move.

THE QUEEN

The queen is a combination of the rook and the bishop: It can move as many spaces as it likes along a rank, a file, or a diagonal. You can see all of the ways a queen can move on the board here.

THE KING

The king is exactly like the queen, except that, unfortunately, he's not as powerful as his "wife." He can move in any direction, but only for one box:

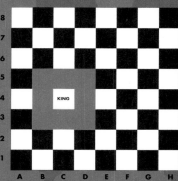

THE KNIGHT

Okay, now things will start to get a little bit sticky. The knight can move only in an L-shape. This means that it moves a total of three boxes: 2 straight, 1 sideways; or 1 straight, 2 sideways. This definitely needs an example:

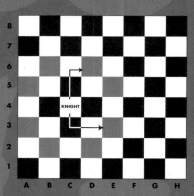

This may be confusing at first, but you'll get the hang of it! Practice by putting the knight anywhere on the board and envisioning all of the places where it can move.

What's special about the knight is that it's the only **major** piece (one from the back row of your board) that can *jump* over other pieces to land in an empty square. It doesn't matter whether that piece is your own or your opponent's; as long as your knight lands in an empty square, your move is legal.

THE PAWN

The pawns are the first line of defense for your beloved king, but you have so many of them that they are basically your least valuable pieces. In fact, they are so weak that they can only move one space forward. That's it. They can't move backward, sideways, diagonal, jump over other pieces, or do anything else fun. Only one space forward. Poor pawns.

There are THREE exceptions to this rule:
1. If a pawn is coming out of its box for the first time, you have the option to move it either one or two spaces. It's up to you.
2. When a pawn captures another piece, it can ONLY capture it by moving one box forward in a diagonal. It can't capture a piece head-on. See the chessboard below for an example:

3. When your pawn reaches the opposite end of the board, it gets a **promotion**. This means that it can become any piece it wants to be, getting that piece's rules, powers, and dental plan. Here's a word of advice: Promote your pawn into a queen. What's the benefit of this move? Well, of course, then you will have two queens (or, if you've lost your queen at any point in the game, this is your chance to gain it back). In fact, if you get every pawn to the opposite end of the board, you could be playing with nine queens at a time (the original, plus your eight promoted pawns).

OBJECTIVE

The object of the game is very simple: Your goal is to capture your opponent's king. But before you do so, you have to be polite enough to give him a warning. There are three different instances in which a king can be threatened: **check**, **stalemate**, and **checkmate.**

CHECK

This is when your opponent's king is being threatened. Once you have checked your opponent's king, he or she must respond by either capturing the attacker, blocking the attacker, or moving his or her king. Otherwise, game over.

STALEMATE

A stalemate is really a fancy way of saying "tie game." It's when your king is in a safe square, but if you move out of it, then your king gets captured. Since you're not allowed to pass a turn in the game of chess, a stalemate is declared.

CHECKMATE

A checkmate, of course, is when you have successfully captured your opponent's king, or vice versa.

STRATEGY

Here are some tips that will help you to improve your game:

Get control of the center squares.
The middle four squares on the board (D4, D5, E4, and E5) are the most important squares on the board because they let you control everything that's going on.

Don't expose your good pieces too early.
You don't want to risk losing a queen or a rook early on. They're too darn valuable. So take your time in taking them out of their homes.

Knights are good for attacking.
Because knights can jump over pieces, they make for good attackers. So don't be shy about bringing them out early. They're usually the first major pieces that a player will bring out of the back row.

Think teamwork.
Don't just move a piece for the sake of moving it. Formulate a plan before taking your turn. Will your move make other, more valuable pieces vulnerable? Will it actually do any good? The secret is that very rarely will a piece do anything by itself. Always think of your pieces as being part of your team.

Practice.
It's very important that you practice as much as possible, as well as read as many chess books as possible. Once you've started playing enough, you'll naturally start to see patterns emerge. You won't even have to think about how a piece moves.

TIC-TAC-TOE

You know the rules. Now get set to play it without a pen. On the opposite page is a tic-tac-toe board that you can use again and again.

RULES

This game is for two players. Each player should pick a checker color. Once you have determined who will go first, the first player can put one of his or her checkers anywhere on the board. Now, each player takes turns trying to get three pieces in a row horizontally, vertically, or diagonally.

HiNt: Use the center square!

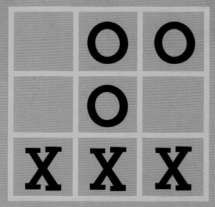

MEMORY MATCHUP

Here's a game that will test your memory. Have a look at the game board on the opposite page—you'll note that there are two of every icon. Then grab a pair of scissors and a sheet of scrap paper. Cut the paper into 16 squares that are bigger than the images you see. Give yourself and your opponent a good sixty seconds or so to really take in the board. Now cover up all of the icons with the paper.

Do you think you remember which icons were where? Now's your chance to find out! Taking turns, you and your opponent must uncover two icons at a time. Your goal, of course, is to uncover two identical icons. If you don't, replace the paper over the icons and turn the board over to your opponent. If you do, you get to keep both slips of paper and go again. The goal, of course, is to have the most pieces of paper once the board is clear.

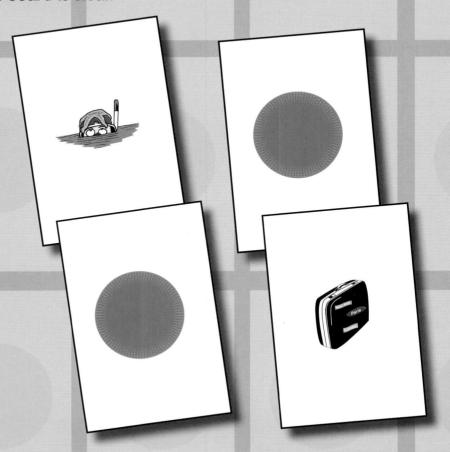

CLASSIC ROAD-TRIP GAMES

Here are a few tried-and-true travel games that require no setup, no equipment, and can accommodate as many players as there are travelers on your trip! How perfectly portable!

TWENTY QUESTIONS

Players take turns thinking of an object. Once the player in question has an object in mind, other players ask up to twenty questions to determine what the object is. The person who correctly guesses the object wins and gets to pick the next object. If no one guesses the object, the original player who thought it up is the winner and gets to pick the next object, and so forth.

THE ALPHABET GAME

Players must find, in consecutive order, the letters of the alphabet out the car window or otherwise in their immediate surroundings. The first person to find the entire alphabet wins.

SINGDOWN

Players pick words such as "blue" or "big" or "car." Each player must then brainstorm (on his or her own) as many songs as he or she can think of using the words in question. Players take turns naming songs. If someone names a song you chose before you do, you must cross it off your list! You get one point for every song, and whoever has the most points at the end of the game wins!

TRUTH OR DARE

Players take turns asking each other, "Truth or dare?" If you choose truth, you must answer any question asked of you, truthfully. If you'd rather be dared, you must agree to do whatever you are dared to do (as long as it's safe!).

TRAVEL SCAVENGER HUNT

Keep an eye out for the following items. The first person to spot one of each item wins. Play this game with as many people as you like!

hubcap	"for sale" sign
luggage tag	football field
mirror	gas station
bicycle	boat
hairbrush	train
television	water tower
airplane	mountain
American flag	fast-food restaurant
river	dog
someone wearing a hat	grocery store

FOR SALE

TONGUE TWISTERS

Try these out five times fast!

Six sick slick slim sycamore saplings.

A box of biscuits, a batch of mixed biscuits.

Red lorry, yellow lorry, red lorry, yellow lorry.

Unique New York.

Six thick thistle sticks. Six thick thistles stick.

Toy boat. Toy boat. Toy boat.

The sixth sick sheik's sixth sheep's sick.

Three free throws.

WORD GAMES

These games require no setup or tools, and any number of people can join in the fun!

Group Storytelling

One person in your group begins a story as he or she would like. *But,* that person stops after a sentence or two, allowing the next player to pick up where the story left off. The story continues onward, rotating every few sentences, until everyone has had a chance to contribute to the silliness at least once. Technically, this game has no winner, but you'll all be laughing too much to care.

Two Truths, One Lie

Players take turns offering three stories to the group, two of which are true and one of which is false. The fun is in guessing which of the three outrageous stories is actually true! Whoever guesses correctly first wins the game. If no one guesses, the storyteller is the winner.

What If

More a game of imagination than competition, the object of "What If" is to propose creative questions to your travel mates. Suggestions include:

"What if you could be a superhero—
what power would you choose?"

"What if you could only eat one food for the rest of your life—
what would it be?"

"What if you were stranded on a desert island—
what book would you bring?"

Have fun coming up with your own questions! The sky's the limit!

WEI QI / GO

Wei Qi, also called Go, is generally believed to be at least three thousand years old, making it one of the world's oldest strategic board games. There are many different stories about the origin of the game, several of which state that various Chinese emperors invented the game as a means of entertaining their sons.

Did you KNOW? There is even a theory that the game was once used by astrologers to divine the future!

RULES OF THE GAME

One of the reasons why Wei Qi is so appealing is that it isn't very complicated. We've provided an especially easy-to-follow variation here. Choose which player will be red and which will be black. Once you've got that sorted out, gather up your checkers.

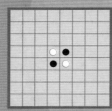

When you've got your checkers in hand, each player places two pieces on the board as shown on the left.

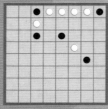

Taking turns, each player places a checker on the board so that it traps an opponent's piece, or pieces. The trapping can be done horizontally, vertically, or diagonally.

Once trapped, the opponent's checker is removed and replaced with one of the trapper's checkers.

If you are unable to trap your opponent, your turn is forfeited and your opponent moves again. If you can make a move, you must take it. A trap must be caused by a move.

When neither player can move, the game is over. The player with the most checkers wins.

OPTICAL ILLUSIONS

An optical illusion is an image that tricks your brain into thinking it's seeing something that's not really there! Check out the phenomenon with the classic optical illusions below:

1. Is this object physically possible? Check again!

2. Do these stairs keep climbing?

3. Believe it or not, the top length of each of these figures is the exact same size!

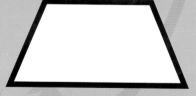

4. Which do you see—the letter *E*, or just black lines?

5. Can you see all three faces?

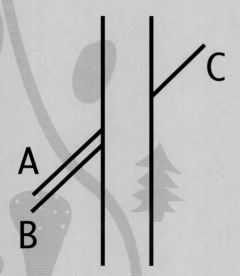

6. Line B is actually the line that connects to line C!

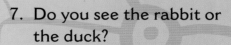

7. Do you see the rabbit or the duck?

PYRAMID SOLITAIRE

Here's a game you can play all by yourself! On the board on the opposite page, place checkers (any color) on the following sixteen spots:

```
5
9  10  11
15  16  17  18  19
21  22  23  24  25  26  27
```

Every move you make has to be a jump over another checker (just like in the original game of checkers). When you jump a piece, remove it from the board. Jumps can be horizontal or vertical, but never diagonal.

Try to jump until there is a single checker left in spot seventeen. Can you do it in just fifteen jumps?

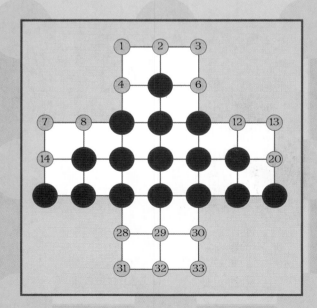

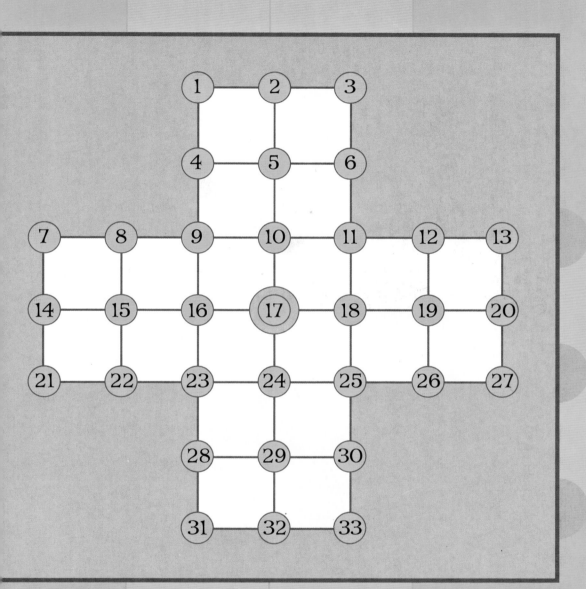

43

TRAVEL SCRAPBOOK

These pages are designed for you to create your own mini-scrapbook of the trips that you take. Every time you travel, fill in the blank spaces below and decorate the page by gluing or taping down souvenirs from your trips: photos, airplane tickets, programs from plays or museums—just use your imagination to make your own memories!

Date: _____

Place Visited: _____

Traveled With: _____

Most Interesting Sight: _____

Most Fun Activity: _____

Best Reason to Visit this Place: _____

Would I Like to Come Back Here? _____

Microsoft® Project 2003

Level 2

Chris Blocher

Jeannine P Pray

Microsoft® Project 2003: Level 2

Part Number: 084726
Course Edition: 1.03

ACKNOWLEDGMENTS

Project Team

Curriculum Developer and Technical Writer: Cindy Caldwell and Jeannine Pray • **Content Manager:** Susan B. SanFilippo • **Content Editors:** Angie J. French and Laura Telford • **Material Editor:** Elizabeth Fuller and Frank Wosnick • **Print Designer:** Isolina Salgado Toner • **Project Technical Specialist:** Michael Toscano

NOTICES

DISCLAIMER: While Element K Courseware LLC takes care to ensure the accuracy and quality of these materials, we cannot guarantee their accuracy, and all materials are provided without any warranty whatsoever, including, but not limited to, the implied warranties of merchantability or fitness for a particular purpose. The name used in the data files for this course is that of a fictitious company. Any resemblance to current or future companies is purely coincidental. We do not believe we have used anyone's name in creating this course, but if we have, please notify us and we will change the name in the next revision of the course. Element K is an independent provider of integrated training solutions for individuals, businesses, educational institutions, and government agencies. Use of screenshots, photographs of another entity's products, or another entity's product name or service in this book is for editorial purposes only. No such use should be construed to imply sponsorship or endorsement of the book by, nor any affiliation of such entity with Element K.

TRADEMARK NOTICES Element K and the Element K logo are trademarks of Element K LLC.

Microsoft Office Project Professional 2003 is a registered trademark of Microsoft Corporation in the U.S. and other countries; the Microsoft products and services discussed or described may be trademarks of Microsoft Corporation. All other product names and services used throughout this book may be common law or registered trademarks of their respective proprietors.

Copyright © 2008 Element K Content LLC. All rights reserved. Screenshots used for illustrative purposes are the property of the software proprietor. This publication, or any part thereof, may not be reproduced or transmitted in any form or by any means, electronic or mechanical, including photocopying, recording, storage in an information retrieval system, or otherwise, without express written permission of Element K, 500 Canal View Boulevard, Rochester, NY 14623, (585) 240-7500, (800) 434-3466. Element K Courseware LLC's World Wide Web site is located at **www.elementkcourseware.com**.

This book conveys no rights in the software or other products about which it was written; all use or licensing of such software or other products is the responsibility of the user according to terms and conditions of the owner. Do not make illegal copies of books or software. If you believe that this book, related materials, or any other Element K materials are being reproduced or transmitted without permission, please call 1-800-478-7788.

Microsoft, the Microsoft Office Logo, PowerPoint, and Outlook are trademarks or registered trademarks of Microsoft Corporation in the United States and/or other countries, and the Microsoft Office Specialist Logo is used under license from owner.

Element K is independent from Microsoft Corporation, and not affiliated with Microsoft in any manner. This publication may be used in assisting students to prepare for a Microsoft Office Specialist Exam. Neither Microsoft, its designated program administrator or courseware reviewer, nor Element K warrants that use of this publication will ensure passing the relevant exam.

HELP US IMPROVE OUR COURSEWARE

Your comments are important to us. Please contact us at Element K Press LLC, 1-800-478-7788, 500 Canal View Boulevard, Rochester, NY 14623, Attention: Product Planning, or through our Web site at **http://support.elementkcourseware.com**.

MICROSOFT® PROJECT 2003: LEVEL 2

CONTENTS

ABOUT THIS COURSE

Microsoft Project 2003: Level 2 is the second course in the Microsoft Project 2003 series. In *Microsoft Project 2003: Level 1* , you used your project management skills to create a complete project plan. This course will build upon that knowledge, and give you the opportunity to work with a project plan once it has entered the project implementation phase.

To successfully deliver a quality product on time and within budget, and to communicate effectively with a project's stakeholders and team members, you need to monitor and modify your plan regularly to compensate for any bumps in the road. This course will help you learn how to do that. You finished planning your project, got buy-in from all the stakeholders, and distributed the assignments to the necessary resources. You decide that you don't need to check your plan until the due date. The due date comes six months later and you decide it's time to close the plan. You begin updating its progress only to discover that barely 50 percent of the project is complete and half of that was done incorrectly. Your clients scream at your boss, your boss screams at you, you scream at the plan's team members! What went wrong? Everyone agreed on the plan and assignments, so why didn't they do their jobs? The fact is, you didn't do your job. Project initiation and planning is only half the battle. Project plans don't monitor themselves; they require constant vigilance. Once a plan gets underway, circumstances often arise that can affect your team's ability to meet deadlines.

Course Description

Target Student

This course is designed for a person who has an understanding of project management concepts, who is responsible for creating and modifying project plans, and who needs a tool to manage those project plans. It is also intended for a person who has a basic understanding of Microsoft Project 2003.

Course Prerequisites

Students enrolling in this class should have:

- An understanding of project management concepts.
- Knowledge of a Windows operating system.
- *Microsoft Project 2003: Level 1.*

The following Element K courses would be helpful, but are not required:

- Project Management Fundamentals
- Harvard Manage Mentor Project Management (online course)
- Project Management Fundamentals Part 1 and 2 (online course)

Knowledge of Microsoft Office 2003 applications would also be helpful.

How to Use This Book

As a Learning Guide

Each lesson covers one broad topic or set of related topics. Lessons are arranged in order of increasing proficiency with *Microsoft Project 2003*; skills you acquire in one lesson are used and developed in subsequent lessons. For this reason, you should work through the lessons in sequence.

We organized each lesson into results-oriented topics. Topics include all the relevant and supporting information you need to master *Microsoft Project 2003*, and activities allow you to apply this information to practical hands-on examples.

You get to try out each new skill on a specially prepared sample file. This saves you typing time and allows you to concentrate on the skill at hand. Through the use of sample files, hands-on activities, illustrations that give you feedback at crucial steps, and supporting background information, this book provides you with the foundation and structure to learn *Microsoft Project 2003* quickly and easily.

As a Review Tool

Any method of instruction is only as effective as the time and effort you are willing to invest in it. In addition, some of the information that you learn in class may not be important to you immediately, but it may become important later on. For this reason, we encourage you to spend some time reviewing the topics and activities after the course. For additional challenge when reviewing activities, try the What You Do column before looking at the How You Do It column.

As a Reference

The organization and layout of the book make it easy to use as a learning tool and as an after-class reference. You can use this book as a first source for definitions of terms, background information on given topics, and summaries of procedures.

Course Objectives

In this course, you will exchange project plan data with other applications, update project plans, create custom reports, and reuse project plan information.

You will:

- exchange project plan data with other applications.
- update a project plan.

- create custom reports.
- reuse existing project plan information.

Course Requirements

Hardware

To use Microsoft Office Project Professional 2003 on each student's machine, you need the following hardware:

- Pentium 233 MHz or higher processor.
- 128 megabytes (MB) of RAM or more.
- 612 megabytes (MB) of available hard-disk space or more.
- CD-ROM drive.
- Super VGA or higher resolution monitor.
- Microsoft Mouse, Microsoft IntelliMouse®, or a compatible pointing device.
- Additional items or services are required to use certain features: 14.4 Kbps or faster modem, and a multimedia computer to access sound and other multimedia effects.

Software

Software required on each student machine includes the following:
- Microsoft Windows XP Professional.
- Microsoft Office Project Professional 2003.
- Microsoft Office Professional Edition 2003.
- Internet Explorer 6.0 with Service Pack 1 or later, if you wish to access the Microsoft Office Project help files on the Internet.

Class Setup

On Each Student Machine:

In order for the class to run properly, perform the following procedures:

This course was written using Microsoft Office Project Professional 2003. However, this course can be keyed using Microsoft Office Project Standard 2003.

1. Install Windows XP Professional.
2. Perform a Complete install of Microsoft Office Project Professional 2003.
3. Perform a Complete Installation of Microsoft Office 2003.
4. Log on as Administrator.

5. Verify that file extensions are visible. (In Windows Explorer, choose Tools→Folder Options and select the View tab. If necessary, uncheck the Hide Extensions For Known File Types option and click OK.)

6. Install a print driver of your choice.

7. The sample data requires that the system date be set to August 1, 2005. In the system tray, double-click the clock. In the Date and Time Properties dialog box, set the date to August 1, 2005, and then click OK. Perform this step on all student and instructor machines.

If your book did not come with a CD, please go to **http://www.elementk.com/courseware-file-downloads** *to download the data files.*

8. On the course CD-ROM, open the 084_726 folder. Then, open the Data folder. Run the 084726dd.exe self-extracting file located within. This will install a folder named 084726Data on your C drive. This folder contains all the data files that you will use to complete this course. Copy all of the data files to the My Documents folder.

9. Launch Microsoft Office Project 2003.

List of Additional Files

Printed with each activity is a list of files students open to complete that activity. Many activities also require additional files that students do not open, but are needed to support the file(s) students are working with. These supporting files are included with the student data files on the course CD-ROM or data disk. Do not delete these files.

LESSON 1

Exchanging Project Plan Data with Other Applications

Lesson Time
1 hour(s)

Lesson Objectives:

In this lesson, you will exchange project plan data with other applications.

You will:

* Import a task list from an Excel file into a new project plan using the Import Wizard.

* Create a custom import map to import resource information from an Access database into an existing project plan.

* Export project plan cost data to an Excel workbook using the Export Wizard.

* Copy a Gantt Chart into a Word document.

* Save project plan information as a Web page.

Introduction

With your project plan file created in the Project Initiation and Project Planning phases, the file now becomes your plan's focal point, with essentially three "masters" to serve—the project manager (you), stakeholders (clients and management), and team members (resources). Each master will often require different things from the plan. In this lesson, you will learn how Project can help you meet these often wide-ranging requirements.

Being able to exchange data efficiently between Project and other applications can save you time while avoiding the potential for mistakes. For instance, a resource provides you with a Microsoft Excel spreadsheet with a task list in it. You could just retype the task list into the plan, but that would be a waste of time and with the potential for making typographical errors. Fortunately, Project can bring the Excel list into the plan exactly as it is. In addition to getting information into a project plan, Project offers you flexibility for quickly getting project information out of a plan in a variety of file formats. If clients don't know how to use Microsoft Project, for example, Project can supply them with the plan details they want in a Word document.

TOPIC A

Import a Task List from an Excel File into a New Project Plan

Team members will often supply you with task lists entered in Excel workbooks because they may not know how to use Project or they may not have a copy of the application. If this is the case, you can use these Excel files to give yourself a head start. In this topic, you will learn how to import a task list from an Excel workbook into a new project plan.

You can bring Excel data into a project plan exactly as it is without ever having to retype a single word. This can give you a significant head start on creating a new project plan.

Importing

Besides its own file format, Project can open, or *import*, task, resource, or assignment data from other file formats into new or existing project plans. The Open dialog box is the starting point for importing file formats such as Access databases, Excel workbooks, and tab-delimited text files. When opening a file format other than a Project file, Project uses its Import Wizard to read the *source file*, the location containing the data to be imported, and to anticipate where the information would best fit in a project, sometimes called the *destination file*. The Import Wizard automatically begins when you attempt to open a file format other than a Project file. The Import Wizard can import selected data or an entire file into either an entirely new project plan or as additions to an existing, open project plan. Once data is imported into Project, there's no connection to the original file. For instance, once you import data from an Excel file using the Import Wizard, updating the data in Project will have no effect on the data in the original Excel file.

Import Maps

The Import Wizard uses a set of instructions called a *map* to tell Project the type of data that is to be imported (task, resource, and assignment-related data), as well as where the data will be imported into a plan. Project comes with some standard import maps ready for you to use in typical importing scenarios, like importing data to create a top-level task list.

Project-Related Templates in Excel

When you install Microsoft Project on a computer that already has Excel on it, Project installs a couple of Excel templates for beginning project plans or task lists in Excel to make the data transition between Excel and Project very straightforward. If you plan on importing either a project plan or a task list from Excel, it's to your benefit to use these templates for the best importing results.

How to Import a Task List from an Excel File into a New Project Plan

Procedure Reference:

To import an Excel task list based on a Project Excel template into a new project plan:

1. Start Project.

2. Choose File→Open.

3. From the Files Of Type drop-down list, select Microsoft Excel Workbooks (*.xls).

4. Open the Excel workbook you want to import.

5. Select Project Excel Template as the data format to be imported.

6. Select As A New Project.

7. Click Finish.

ACTIVITY 1-1

Importing an Excel Task List into a New Project Plan

Data Files:

- CSS Task List.xls

Setup:

Your computer is running, and all applications and data files have been properly installed. CSS Task List.xls is in the My Documents folder.

Scenario:

You're ready to begin a new training manual project to teach people how to use Cascading Style Sheets (CSS), and your manager has supplied you with an Excel file named CSS Task List.xls. It's a very basic task list that she created in Excel using the Microsoft Project Task List Import template. It only contains task names and some of her notes. (See Figure 1-1.) The new project plan's Entry table should look like Figure 1-2 once you've finished.

CSS is a method used to control Web page formatting.

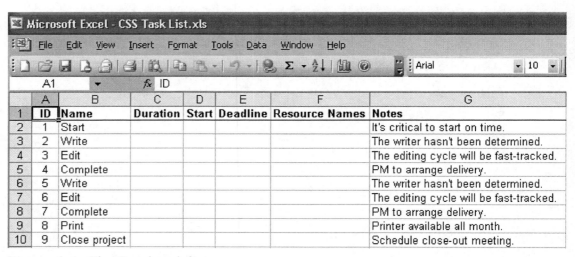

Figure 1-1: *The Excel task list.*

	🕔	Task Name	Duration	Start	Finish
1		Start	1 day	Mon 11/3/03	Mon 11/3/03
2		Write	1 day	Mon 11/3/03	Mon 11/3/03
3		Edit	1 day	Mon 11/3/03	Mon 11/3/03
4		Complete	1 day	Mon 11/3/03	Mon 11/3/03
5		Write	1 day	Mon 11/3/03	Mon 11/3/03
6		Edit	1 day	Mon 11/3/03	Mon 11/3/03
7		Complete	1 day	Mon 11/3/03	Mon 11/3/03
8		Print	1 day	Mon 11/3/03	Mon 11/3/03
9		Close project	1 day	Mon 11/3/03	Mon 11/3/03

Figure 1-2: *The imported task list in the Gantt Chart view's Entry table.*

What You Do	How You Do It
1. **Open the CSS Task List Excel file in Project.**	a. **Choose File→Open.**
	b. If necessary, **navigate to the My Documents folder.**
	c. From the Files Of Type drop-down list, **select Microsoft Excel Workbooks (*.xls).**

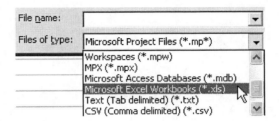

	d. **Select CSS Task List.xls.**
	e. **Click Open** to launch the Import Wizard.
2. The format of the data to be imported is a Project Excel template. **Import the file as a new project and compare your results to Figure 1-2.**	a. **Click Next.**
	b. **Select Project Excel Template and click Next.**
	c. **Verify that As A New Project is selected and click Finish.**
	d. **Compare your results to Figure 1-2.**

3. **In Gantt Chart view of the new project plan, where did Project import the contents that were in Excel's Name column?**

4. **Where did Project import the contents that were in Excel's Notes column?**

5. **Notice the Indicators column. What did Project place on each task?**

✐ You may want to remove or modify these constraints in the Task Information dialog box to suit your plan.

---

6. Based on your knowledge of what is generally required in a project plan, what elements still need to be entered and/or completed before you begin using this new plan?

---

7. Save the project plan as *My CSS Project Plan.mpp*.

    a. Choose File→Save As.

    b. In the Save As dialog box, **verify that the contents of the My Documents folder are displayed.**

    c. In the File Name drop-down list box, **type *My CSS Project Plan***

    d. **Click Save.**

TOPIC B

Create a Custom Import Map

Not all the information that you receive will be stored in a readily importable file. Nor will you always want every bit of data from a file given to you. More often than not, you will want to be able to extract only the data you want from a variety of file formats. In this topic, you will create a custom import map to help you accomplish this.

Besides the benefits you would ordinarily have from importing an entire file into a plan—saving time and avoiding new typing mistakes—being able to pick and choose the data you want to import has another upside: you don't waste time deleting extraneous information from the plan. For instance, when you import an entire file into a plan, *all* of its information comes in—even stuff you don't want. Then you're stuck picking through the plan, deleting unnecessary items. By selectively importing data, you can avoid this added chore, as well as the potential problem of accidentally deleting some necessary data.

Fields

Definition:

In Project, a *field* is a location in a chart, form, or sheet that contains a unique type of information relating to an assignment, resource, or task. Typically, fields are displayed as columns in the various Project tables.

Example:

In the Gantt Chart view, for instance, each column in the Entry table is considered a field (see Figure 1-3). Similarly, database applications, such as Microsoft Access, store fields of unique data in tables, where each database table contains columns of related fields.

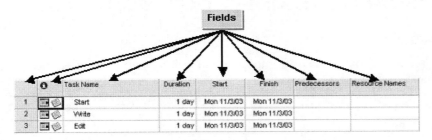

Figure 1-3: *Fields in the Entry table.*

Custom Import Maps

Although Project's default import data maps may be helpful in certain situations, for the most part, you are more likely to create your own custom maps. As shown in Figure 1-4, the Import Wizard lets you create *custom import maps* to determine exactly which pieces of data are to be imported from the source file, as well as where the data will be located in the destination file project plan; this is called mapping the source file data to the destination file project plan. Not every field needs to be mapped, though. When fields being imported have identically named fields in Project, the Import Wizard will do the mapping for you—see the Notes fields in Figure 1-4, for instance. Both the Access table and the project plan have fields named "Notes." Because the field names are identical, the Import Wizard automatically mapped the fields to each other. (See the Preview area of the Import Wizard dialog box in Figure 1-4.) Source file data that remains unmapped will not be imported into the destination file project plan. These custom maps can be saved for future use if desired. Think of a custom import map as a grocery list. The source file data is the store and your shopping cart is the destination file project plan. When you go to the store, you don't put every item in your cart. You pick and choose only those items you want to buy.

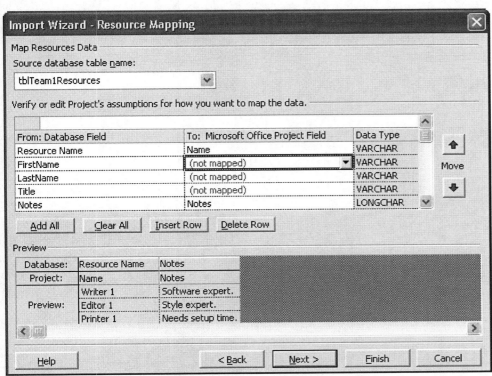

Figure 1-4: *Map from database fields (left) to Microsoft Project fields (right).*

How to Create a Custom Import Map

Procedure Reference:

To create a custom import map to import resource information from an Access database into an existing project plan:

1. Open the project plan that will contain the imported data, if necessary.

2. From within Project, open the Access database to start the Import Wizard.

3. Click Next.

4. If necessary, select New Map.

5. Click Next.

6. Select Append The Data To The Active Project.

   ✐ You can also choose to merge the data into the active project as well.

7. Click Next.

8. Check the type of data you want to import (Tasks, Resources, or Assignments).

9. Click Next.

10. Select the database table that contains the data you want to import.

11. Choose the names of the database fields you want to import and then map them to the corresponding Microsoft Project fields that will receive the imported data.

12. Verify that only the information you want to import is displayed in the Preview area. (Insert or delete rows of fields as needed.)

13. Save the custom import map if desired, and click Finish.

ACTIVITY 1-2

Creating a Custom Import Map

Data Files:

• Resource Teams.mdb

Setup:

The project plan My CSS Project Plan.mpp is open in Gantt Chart view. (The project plan doesn't contain any resources.) The Resource Teams.mdb Access database is located in the My Documents folder.

Scenario:

It's time to add resources to the My CSS Project Plan file. A few months ago, you divided your department resources into four teams and created an Access database named Resource Teams.mdb to store pertinent information about each team. In this plan's Resource Sheet, you want to use some of the resource information for Team 1—the Resource Name and Notes database fields. When you've successfully imported the database fields into the plan, your Resource Sheet will look like Figure 1-5.

	ⓘ	Resource Name	Type	Material Label	Initials	Group	Max. Units	Std. Rate	Ovt. Rate	Cost/Use	Accrue At	Base Calendar
1		Writer 1	Work		W		100%	$0.00/hr	$0.00/hr	$0.00	Prorated	Standard
2		Editor 1	Work		E		100%	$0.00/hr	$0.00/hr	$0.00	Prorated	Standard
3		Printer 1	Work		P		100%	$0.00/hr	$0.00/hr	$0.00	Prorated	Standard
4		Artist 1	Work		A		100%	$0.00/hr	$0.00/hr	$0.00	Prorated	Standard
5		Project Manager 1	Work		P		100%	$0.00/hr	$0.00/hr	$0.00	Prorated	Standard
6		Staff Assistant 1	Work		S		100%	$0.00/hr	$0.00/hr	$0.00	Prorated	Standard
7		Account Rep 1	Work		A		100%	$0.00/hr	$0.00/hr	$0.00	Prorated	Standard
8		Publisher 1	Work		P		100%	$0.00/hr	$0.00/hr	$0.00	Prorated	Standard
9		Subject Matter Expert	Work		S		100%	$0.00/hr	$0.00/hr	$0.00	Prorated	Standard

Figure 1-5: *My CSS Project Plan's Resource Sheet with fields imported from Access.*

What You Do	How You Do It
1. **Open the Resource Teams Access database in Project.**	a. **Choose File→Open.**
	b. From the Files Of Type drop-down list, **select Microsoft Access Databases (*.mdb).**

What You Do	How You Do It
	c. From the My Documents folder, **select Resource Teams.mdb.**
	d. **Click Open** to launch the Import Wizard.

2. Create a new map so that the data is appended to the active project, My CSS Project Plan.mpp.

   a. Click Next.

   b. If necessary, **select New Map and click Next.**

   c. If necessary, **select Append The Data To The Active Project and click Next.**

   d. As the type of data you want to import, **check Resources and click Next.**

3. From the Team 1 Resources table, **map the Resource Name field to Project's Name field.**

   a. Below the Map Resources Data heading, from the Source Database Table Name drop-down list, **select tblTeam1Resources.**

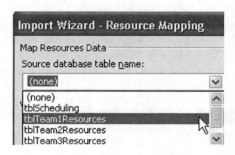

   b. In the From: Database Field list, **select Resource Name.**

   c. In the To: Microsoft Office Project Field list, to the right of the Resource Name field, **select (not mapped).**

From: Database Field	To: Microsoft Office Project Field
EmployeeID	(not mapped)
Department	(not mapped)
Resource Name	(not mapped)
FirstName	(not mapped)

   d. **Type** *Name* **and press Enter.**

4. Scroll down the field list.

   Are any database fields already mapped to Project fields?

5. Finish the Import Wizard and compare the Resource Sheet in My CSS Project Plan to Figure 1-5.

    a. **Click Next.** The Import Wizard gives you the opportunity to save the custom import map you just created. However, we won't be reusing it again.

    b. **Click Finish without saving the map.**

         At this point, you could save the map for future use, if desired.

    c. If necessary, **switch to the Resource Sheet view.**

    d. **Compare the Resource Sheet in My CSS Project Plan.mpp to Figure 1-5.**

6. From the database, where did Project import the Resource Name and Notes fields?

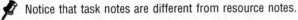 Notice that task notes are different from resource notes.

7. **Were any unwanted database fields imported? For instance, was data from the database's Department, First Name, Last Name, or Title fields added to the plan's Resource Sheet?**

8. **Close My CSS Project Plan, saving changes as needed.**

    a. **Choose File→Close.**

    b. **Click Yes** to save changes if prompted.

TOPIC C

Export Project Plan Cost Data into Excel

Project can act as a sort of data turnstile. Not only can it import data from other applications, but it can export project plan data so that it can be used by other applications, such as Excel. In this topic, you will learn how to export data into an Excel workbook.

Why would you ever want to save data out of a project plan once it's in there? Simple. Besides the obvious fact that not everyone has or knows how to use Project, when it comes to number crunching, Project's calculating power cannot compare to Excel. Being able to export data lets you use the right tool for the job.

Exporting

Unlike importing, which takes data into a project plan, *exporting* copies data out of a project plan and stores it as a different file format, such as Excel workbooks, Access databases, or tab-delimited text files. From the Save As dialog box, saving project data as a different file type triggers Project's Export Wizard. Using data maps, whether they are supplied by Project or custom maps that you create, the Export Wizard determines the type of data being exported and where that data should be stored in the destination file. Similar to importing data, once data is exported from a source file project plan to a new destination file format, no connection remains between the two files. If you update the project plan, you will need to export the updated information again.

How to Export Project Plan Cost Data into Excel

Procedure Reference:

To export project plan cost data into an Excel file using the Export Wizard and an existing data map:

1. Open the project plan that contains the cost information to be exported.

2. Choose File→Save As, name the file, and select Excel Workbook from the Save As Type drop-down list.

3. Click Save to start the Export Wizard.

4. If necessary, select Selected Data and click Next.

5. Select Use Existing Map and click Next.

6. Choose a map for your data and click Next.

7. Select the types of data to be exported and any Excel options you want and click Next.

8. Modify data field mapping if desired and click Next.

9. Click Finish to export the data.

ACTIVITY 1-3

Exporting Project Plan Cost Data to an Excel File

Data Files:

- CSS Book.mpp

Setup:

Project is running, but no files are open.

Scenario:

Steve from Accounting needs to know right away what the anticipated total cost will be for developing the Cascading Style Sheets training manual. In addition, he needs the total cost broken down by individual tasks by tomorrow. When you offer to email him the project plan file so he can get what he needs himself, he quickly replies that he doesn't have Project on his machine, and what he really needs is the cost data in an Excel workbook so he can run some calculations on it before adding it to the next quarter's budget. Once the cost data has been exported, open the workbook in Excel to verify that your exported data looks like Figure 1-6.

📌 If you see ### in any of the cells, widen the column to display the numbers.

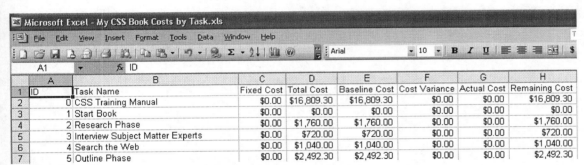

Figure 1-6: *Exported project plan cost data in an Excel workbook.*

What You Do	How You Do It
1. In the CSS Book project plan, **display the Cost table in Task Sheet view.**	a. From the My Documents folder, **open CSS Book.mpp.**
	b. **Choose View→More Views.**
	c. In the More Views dialog box, **select Task Sheet and click Apply.**
	d. **Choose View→Table:Entry→Cost.**
2. What's the estimated total cost for the CSS Book project?	

3.	Start the Export Wizard, saving the plan's cost data to an Excel workbook named *My CSS Book Costs By Task.xls*.	a.	Choose File→Save As.
		b.	Name the file *My CSS Book Costs By Task*
		c.	From the Save As Type drop-down list, **select Microsoft Excel Workbook (*.xls).**
		d.	**Click Save** to start the Export Wizard.
4.	Export selected data using the existing map named Cost Data By Task. Make sure the exported task data includes headers in the Excel file before you accept all of the default mappings.	a.	**Click Next.**
		b.	If necessary, **select the Selected Data option and click Next.**
		c.	**Select Use Existing Map and click Next.**
		d.	**Select the existing data map named Cost Data By Task and click Next.**
		e.	If necessary, **check both the Tasks and Export Includes Headers options and click Next.**
		f.	To accept the default field mappings, **click Next and finish the Export Wizard.**

The data will be stored in a worksheet named Task Costs.

5. Open the My CSS Book Costs By Task Excel workbook. It should look like **Figure 1-6.** When you're satisfied with the exported results, **exit Excel without saving changes.**

a. **Choose Start→All Programs→Microsoft Office→Microsoft Office Excel 2003.**

> If you are using Windows 2000, choose Start→Programs→Microsoft Office→Microsoft Office Excel 2003.

b. **Click the Open button.**

c. In the My Documents folder, **double-click My CSS Book Costs By Task.xls** to open it.

d. If necessary, **adjust column widths to display all the exported data.**

e. **Compare the workbook to Figure 1-6.** The available task cost data should be entered. Since the project hasn't started yet, Cost Variance and Actual Cost are set at $0.00.

f. In Excel, **choose File→Exit.** If prompted to save changes, **click No** to close the workbook and exit the application.

TOPIC D

Copy a Picture into a Word Document

Exporting is a great way to get data out of a plan, but what if you want to send someone a picture of a Gantt Chart or show someone a picture of a resource graph? Project lets you create pictures of any view. In this topic, you will see how to copy a picture into a Word document.

Taking pictures of your project plan gives you a quick way to include project plan details in a much wider variety of applications than exporting does. So even though people may not have access to Project or one of the applications that can access exported data, you can still give project information in the form of a picture. You can take a snapshot of any project plan view and either paste it into an open file that can display pictures, such as in a PowerPoint slide show, or save it as a graphic file that you can attach to an email or store in a folder on your computer.

Copy Picture

The Copy Picture button on the Standard toolbar lets you "take a picture" of a project plan's active view, just like you were using a screen-capture program. Whatever is shown on the screen can become part of the picture. For that reason, you should always position the desired information so that it's displayed in the view before you take the picture. It's also important to note that a copied picture is just that, a picture—not text that can be edited or modified. If you want to copy data from a project plan view so that it can be edited in another application, use the normal Copy command (either Edit→Copy or Edit→Copy Cell, depending on what is selected) and paste it into the desired application.

 You can also choose Edit→Copy Picture.

Copy Picture Options

When you invoke the Copy Picture command, the subsequent dialog box (see Figure 1-7) offers many options. First, you must decide upon how you want the image copied, or rendered. If you want to copy information just as it's displayed on the screen—formatting, colors, and all—select the For Screen option. If you want the picture to look like it will when it's printed by your computer's default printer, select the For Printer option. And lastly, if you want to save the picture as a file that can be used in a Web page, choose the To GIF Image File option. (*GIF* stands for Graphics Interchange Format and is a common file format for graphic images on the Web.) Using the Copy options, you can decide whether you want to include all visible rows on the screen in the picture or just those that were selected before you invoked the Copy Picture command. Similarly, the Timescale options let you decide to include just dates shown on the screen or from a time period that you specify. (The Copy and Timescale options are available only in certain views.)

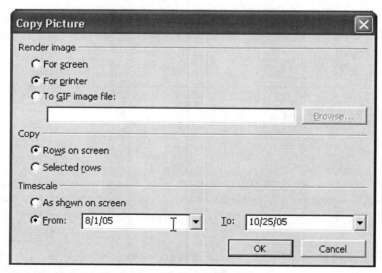

Figure 1-7: *The Copy Picture dialog box.*

How to Copy a Picture into a Word Document

Procedure Reference:

To copy a picture of a project plan view and paste it into a Word document:

1. Display a project plan in the desired view.

2. Position the data you want to include in the picture so that it's displayed on screen.

3. On the Standard toolbar, click the Copy Picture button.

4. Select an appropriate rendering option.

5. Select whether or not you want to include all rows, or just selected ones.

6. Select a time scale, if desired.

7. Click OK.

 The procedure for pasting copied pictures into other applications is similar.

8. Launch Word and open the document that will receive the picture.

9. Place the insertion point in the desired location and paste the copied picture.

ACTIVITY 1-4

Copying a Picture of Gantt Chart View into a Word Document

Data Files:

*   Initial CSS Book Schedule.doc

Setup:

The CSS Book.mpp project plan is open in Task Sheet view.

 If monitor display resolutions are lower than 1024 x 768 pixels, the amount of information captured in the picture will be different than the screens shown in this activity.

Scenario:

Carol Pennelo, one of the project sponsors, wants you to add some information to the Initial CSS Book Schedule.doc file she sent. Before the plan gets underway, she wants a complete task list that identifies task dependencies. She intends to include the information in a document that will be printed and mailed to other sponsors. You decide the best way to provide her with that information is to copy a picture of the entire CSS Book.mpp plan in Gantt Chart view and paste it into the supplied Word document. Your results should be similar to Figure 1-8.

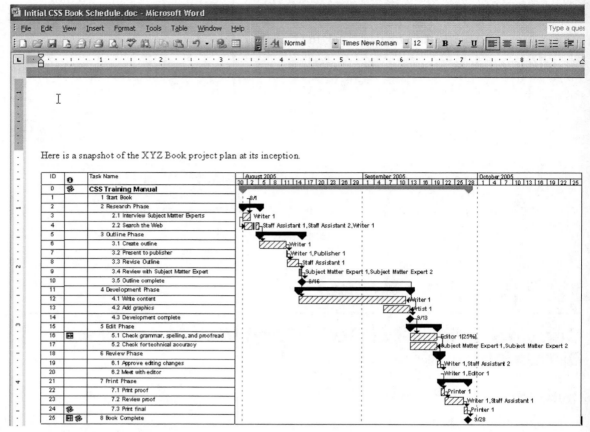

Here is a snapshot of the XYZ Book project plan at its inception.

ID		Task Name	August 2005 / September 2005 / October 2005
0		**CSS Training Manual**	
1		1 Start Book	8/1
2		2 Research Phase	
3		2.1 Interview Subject Matter Experts	Writer 1
4		2.2 Search the Web	Staff Assistant 1,Staff Assistant 2,Writer 1
5		3 Outline Phase	
6		3.1 Create outline	Writer 1
7		3.2 Present to publisher	Writer 1,Publisher 1
8		3.3 Revise Outline	Staff Assistant 1
9		3.4 Review with Subject Matter Expert	Subject Matter Expert 1,Subject Matter Expert 2
10		3.5 Outline complete	8/16
11		4 Development Phase	
12		4.1 Write content	Writer 1
13		4.2 Add graphics	Artist 1
14		4.3 Development complete	9/13
15		5 Edit Phase	
16		5.1 Check grammar, spelling, and proofread	Editor 1[25%]
17		5.2 Check for technical accuracy	Subject Matter Expert 1,Subject Matter Expert 2
18		6 Review Phase	
19		6.1 Approve editing changes	Writer 1,Staff Assistant 2
20		6.2 Meet with editor	Writer 1,Editor 1
21		7 Print Phase	
22		7.1 Print proof	Printer 1
23		7.2 Review proof	Writer 1,Staff Assistant 1
24		7.3 Print final	Printer 1
25		8 Book Complete	9/28

Figure 1-8: *A copied picture of Gantt Chart view pasted into a Word document.*

What You Do	How You Do It
1. Display the CSS Book project plan in Gantt Chart view so the Task Name column is visible in the table and all tasks are visible in the Gantt Chart.	a. Choose View→Gantt Chart and close the Project Guide, if necessary.
If the Task Pane or Project Guide is displayed, you may want to close it so you can see more of the screen.	b. If necessary, adjust the Divide bar so that only the task names are visible in the Entry table.
	c. Use the vertical and horizontal scroll bars so you can see all of the tasks in the Gantt Chart.
	You may want to use the Zoom tools on the Standard toolbar to display more of the Gantt Chart.

2. **Copy a picture of the Gantt Chart view so that all the displayed rows on the screen are rendered for printing with a time scale from 8/1/05 to 10/25/05.**

   📌 Although the plan will be complete by 10/25/05, extending the time scale makes room for longer task labels.

   a. On the Standard toolbar, from the Toolbar Options button, **click the Copy Picture button** to display the Copy Picture dialog box.

   b. In the Render Image area, **select For Printer.**

   c. If necessary, in the Copy area, **select Rows On Screen.**

   d. In the Timescale area's From drop-down list box, **type *8/1/05*** and in the To drop-down list box, **type *10/25/05***

   📌 Even though the plan ends on 9/28/05, the additional time will make room for labels.

   e. **Click OK.** With the picture copied to the clipboard, you're ready to paste it into the Word document.

---

3. **Open the Initial CSS Book Schedule document in Word and paste the copied picture at the end of the document.** Your document should be similar to Figure 1-8.

   a. **Start Microsoft Word** (Start→All Programs→Microsoft Office→Microsoft Office Word 2003).

   📌 If you are using Windows 2000, choose Start→Programs→Microsoft Office→Microsoft Office Word 2003.

   b. From the My Documents folder, **open Initial CSS Book Schedule.doc.**

   c. Using the down arrow key, **move the insertion point to the end of the document.**

   d. **Choose Edit→Paste.** The document should look something like Figure 1-8.

---

4. **In the Word document, can you edit any of the task names?**

 If you accidentally display the Format Picture dialog box, just click Cancel.

5. Save the file as *My Initial CSS Book Schedule.doc* and exit Word.

    a. **Choose File→Save As.**

    b. **Name the file** *My Initial CSS Book Schedule.doc*

    c. **Click Save.**

    d. **Choose File→Exit.**

TOPIC E

Save Project Plan Information as a Web Page

Even though being able to export project plan data in other file formats increases the number of team members who can use the information, the number of applications that can open exported data is still limited. So, is there a way to increase accessibility and utility at the same time? Of course. Perhaps the most useful way to provide project details to the most people is to save plan information as a Web page. In this topic, you will see how to do that.

By saving assignment, resource, and task information as a Web page, the data becomes almost universally accessible. The resulting Web page can be emailed, posted on an intranet, or even on the Internet on your company's Web site. The details can be copied and pasted into any application as needed. You can even include a picture of a view that you captured using the Copy Picture button if you want, so the data is further supported by a visual representation.

How to Save Project Plan Information as a Web Page

Procedure Reference:

To save information from an open project plan as a Web page using an existing map:

1. Choose File→Save As Web Page, name the file, and click Save to start the Export Wizard.

    It's a good idea to keep Web page names as short as possible and without using spaces or odd punctuation.

2. Select Use Existing Map and click Next.

3. Select the Export To HTML Using Standard Template map for your data and click Next.

4. As needed, select the types of data to be exported, change HTML options, and include an image if needed, and then click Next.

> 🖈 If you plan to distribute a Web page that has a graphic in it, be sure to distribute the graphic, too.

5. As needed, modify data mappings for each data type.

6. Click Finish to export the data.

HTML

Short for HyperText Markup Language, *HTML* is the primary markup language for creating Web pages, which is why most Web pages have either an .htm or .html file extension. Since Project creates the Web pages for you, you don't need to know how to write any HTML. Worth knowing, however, is that HTML files can be edited in any application that can open text files. So if you choose to edit a Web page, you can do so without needing any special software.

ACTIVITY 1-5

Saving Project Plan Information as a Web Page

Setup:
The CSS Book.mpp project plan is open.

Scenario:
Although your project sponsors are all off site, they still want to be able to see project plan data on a regular basis without having to pester you for it. Since they have access to your secure intranet, and your IT department can put the Web page on the intranet site for you, you decide that the most effective way to provide the information is to save the project plan as a Web page. The existing HTML data map is exactly what you want—all the assignment, resource, and task data without having to modify any of the mappings. The sponsors will be thrilled when they can get the information so quickly and easily. (Your Web page should look similar to Figure 1-9.)

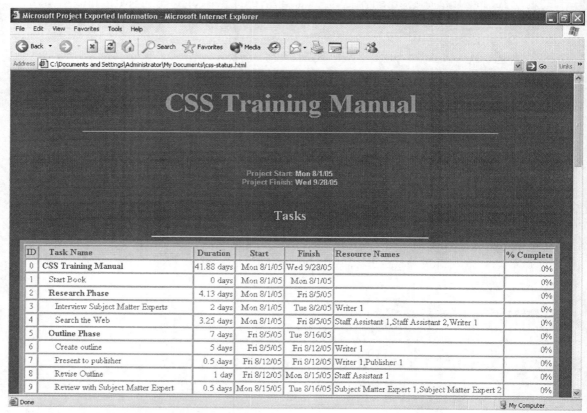

Figure 1-9: *The exported Web page.*

What You Do	How You Do It
1. Save the project plan as a Web page named *css-status.html*.	a. Choose File→Save As Web Page.
	b. Name the file *css-status.html*
	c. Click Save to start the Export Wizard.

2. **Export the project plan information as a Web page.**

   a. **Click Next.**

   b. **Select Use Existing Map and click Next.**

   c. **Select the existing data map named Export To HTML Using Standard Template and click Next.**

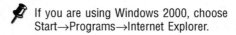 At this point in the Export Wizard, you could include an image file in your Web page.

   d. **To accept all the remaining default settings, click Finish.**

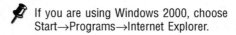 At this point in the Export Wizard, you could modify data mappings for each data type.

---

3. **Open the css-status Web page in your browser.**

   a. **Choose Start→All Programs→Internet Explorer.**

 If you are using Windows 2000, choose Start→Programs→Internet Explorer.

   b. **Choose File→Open.**

   c. **Browse to the My Documents folder and double-click css-status.html.**

   d. **Click OK** to display the Web page in the browser window.

---

4. **What exported project plan information is displayed in the Web page?**

When you're satisfied with the exported results, **close the browser and, in Project, close the CSS Book project plan without saving any changes.**

 All of the Web page data is selectable so they can be copied and pasted into other applications.

Lesson 1 Follow-up

Good work! You have learned the basics of exchanging project plan data between Project and other applications. You can now import information into a project plan, whether it's from an Excel task list or an Access database. In addition to getting information into your plan, you can get information out of it by exporting to a Word document or Web page, or by simply copying a picture into another open application. You're now ready to enter the Project Implementation phase and begin updating a plan.

1.   **On your job, what types of business documents do you frequently encounter that you might be able to import into a project plan? Discuss your answers with the class.**

2.   **Why might you want to save project plan information in applications other than Project?**

LESSON 2
Updating a Project Plan

Lesson Time
2 hour(s)

Lesson Objectives:

In this lesson, you will update a project plan.

You will:

- Update task progress.
- View task progress in a project plan.
- Split a task.
- Reschedule a task.
- Filter tasks in a project plan.
- Save an interim project plan.
- Create a custom table.
- Add a custom column to a custom table.
- Hyperlink a document to a task.

Introduction

Now that you know how to get information into and out of a project plan as needed, you are ready to begin the plan's Project Implementation phase. This is the point where many plans fail because project managers stop here because they think, "The plan is done, everyone knows what they're supposed to be doing and when it's supposed to be done." The reality is that this is when project management begins. This lesson will show you how to keep your project plan up to date.

You need to drive your project plans or they will drive you (into another profession). By continuously monitoring and constantly updating a plan's progress throughout the Project Implementation phase of a project plan's life cycle, you will be better suited to identify potential problems as they arise, or, at the very least, let you take the appropriate measures to get the plan back on track once the problem occurs. This lesson will help you feel more comfortable behind the wheel of your plan by showing you how to steer a plan to its completion in a timely fashion.

TOPIC A

Enter Task Progress Information

As soon as resources begin their assigned tasks, progress of some kind is being made. The trick is to be able to capture that progress information in your project plan. In this topic, you will see how Project provides you with a variety of ways to enter task progress so you can determine whether or not tasks are on schedule.

Someone once asked, "How can you know where you're going if you don't know where you've been?" That question has never been more applicable than when it's asked in the context of managing a project plan. As you know, if a problem arises with a task, that one problem can often trigger a chain reaction of problems—scheduling, added costs, and other factors—in subsequent tasks, unless you handle the problem immediately. Based upon progress data supplied by your resources, you can keep a plan current, so when you see problems arise, you can make just-in-time adjustments to put out small fires before they become roaring infernos. If you fail to update your project plan regularly, you may not catch a problem before it's too late. Your job role can quickly switch from project manager to crisis control officer; your deadline can slip a few days, weeks, months, or even years before you know it, making it impossible to rescue the project. You don't want a project plan to ever reach that point. Being able to identify where you are in a project plan is essential to ensuring your plan's success.

How to Enter Task Progress Information

Procedure Reference:

To enter the task progress information collected from team members in a project plan's Tracking table:

1. Display the Tracking table in Task Sheet view.

2. Enter the collected progress information (percent complete, actual work, and others) in the appropriate fields for each task.

Tracking Toolbar

For updating selected tasks, you might find the Tracking toolbar beneficial (see Figure 2-1). As you might expect, it gives you access to many of Project's tracking tools. To display it, choose View→Toolbars→Tracking. Of all the toolbar's tools, Update Tasks gives you the most flexibility. It lets you update a wide variety of task progress information such as percent complete, actual duration, remaining duration, and actual start and finish dates.

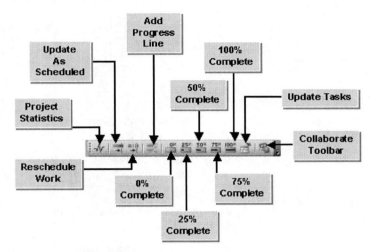

Figure 2-1: *The Tracking toolbar.*

ACTIVITY 2-1

Updating Task Progress in a Project Plan

Data Files:

• CSS Week 1.mpp

Setup:

All files are closed and Project is the active application.

Scenario:

The Cascading Style Sheet (CSS) Training Manual project has been going on for a week now. It's now Monday morning, 8/8/05, and you have talked to the resources that have tasks in progress. They've updated you regarding the progress they've made—see Table 2-1. You are now ready to update the tasks in the CSS Week 1 project plan.

Table 2-1: *Collected Task Progress Data as of 8/8/05*

Task	Progress Data
1 Start Book	The book started on time, so mark it as 100-percent complete.
3 Interview Subject Matter Expert	It's 100-percent complete, but it only lasted 1 day instead of 2.
4 Investigate the Software	The writer has actually worked 32 hours on it.

LESSON 2

What You Do	How You Do It
1. In the CSS Week 1 project plan, **change the current date to *8/8/05*.**	a. **Open CSS Week 1.mpp.**
	b. **Choose Project→Project Information** to display the Project Information dialog box.
For the purposes of this class, to simulate the passing of time, it is critical that you set the current date when instructed to do so.	c. In the Current Date field, **type *8/8/05***
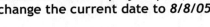 The Current Date gridline is displayed in the Gantt Chart on 8/8/05.	d. **Click OK.**
2. **Use the Tracking table in Task Sheet view to enter Task 1's progress.**	a. **Choose View→More Views.**
	b. From the Views list box, **select Task Sheet and click Apply.**
For this course, a task's ID number is used when referring to individual tasks—not the task's outline number.	c. **Choose View→Table:Entry→Tracking.**
	d. For Task 1, **select the % Complete field.**
	e. **Type *100***
	f. Paying attention to the other fields for Task 1, **press Enter.**

3. **When you pressed Enter, what fields were filled in?**

_____

_____

 Use Edit→Undo Entry and Edit→Redo Entry to help you see the changes as they happen.

4. **Enter progress data for Task 3.**

 Be sure to mark the task 100-percent complete before entering the Actual Duration data.

a. For Task 3, **mark it as 100-percent complete.**

b. **Select the Act. Dur. field.**

c. **Type** *1*

d. Paying attention to the other fields for Task 3, **press Enter.**

5. **When you changed the Actual Duration to 1 day, what fields were affected?**

 How Actual Duration is Calculated.

If you type a value in the % Complete field, Microsoft Office Project 2003 calculates actual duration as follows: Actual Duration = Duration * Percent Complete

If you type a value in the Actual Duration field, Project calculates the Remaining Duration as follows: Remaining Duration = Duration - Actual Duration

If you enter an actual duration greater than the scheduled duration, Project changes scheduled duration to match the new actual duration, sets the remaining duration to zero, and sets the percent complete to 100.

You may want to increase the column width for some fields to view their data.

6. Using data from Table 2-1, **update the number of actual hours worked for Task 4.**

When you changed the Actual Work hours to 32 hours, what fields were affected?

Save the project plan as *My CSS Week 1.mpp*

TOPIC B

View Task Progress

Now that individual task progress data has been entered, it's time to view how the entire plan is coming along. Project provides you with dozens of ways to view task progress; however, the true value of viewing task progress is being able to compare the actual progress to a baseline schedule or cost figure. In this topic, you will see how to make that comparison.

By comparing actual task progress to a plan's baseline information, you can immediately identify if a project plan is on schedule or not. Making this comparison also helps ensure that you have the necessary information to make in-progress adjustments to remaining tasks so you can keep the actuals in sync with the baseline schedule. Keep in mind that just because a plan is progressing, doesn't mean that it's progressing according to schedule. If you don't keep your eye on both actual progress and the project plan's baseline schedule, you may be in for an unpleasant surprise at the end of a project plan.

Tracking Gantt Chart

Displayed in the Tracking Gantt view, the *Tracking Gantt chart* is similar to the ordinary Gantt Chart—both display bars for tasks' currently scheduled start and finish dates. The Tracking Gantt chart has an added benefit, though. Besides bars for scheduled start and finish dates, it also displays bars for baseline start and finish dates. (See Figure 2-2.) Displaying both sets of bars lets you easily determine which tasks are slipping or ahead of schedule.

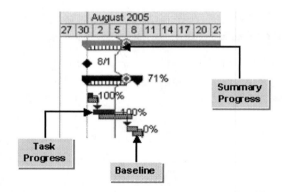

Figure 2-2: *A project plan displayed in Tracking Gantt view.*

Variance Table

For a more complete task progress picture, you can display the Variance table with the Tracking Gantt chart. The *Variance table* shows Start Var. and Finish Var. columns listing the number of days a task is ahead or behind schedule when comparing actual dates to baseline dates. Negative numbers indicate that a task was started or finished early, where a positive number indicates the number of days a task was started late.

Check Progress Pane

If you just need a quick way to identify whether or not a task is on schedule or not, use the *Check Progress pane*. To show the pane, on the Project Guide toolbar, click Track and then click the Check The Progress Of The Project link. This displays the Project Guide: Custom Tracking view. In the table, the Status Indicator shows if a task is late, on schedule, or has been completed.

Status Date

The *status date* is a date that you can specify in a plan's Project Information dialog box. Rather than using the current date, you can set a status date to enter or view progress as of an earlier date that you determine. Typically, project managers set a status date to "go back in time" to enter progress data or to generate reports for a plan's "health" on a particular date. For instance, the current date may be 10/1/04, and you're in the middle of a year-long plan, but you need to know what the status was on 9/1/04. You can set the status date to display that information. By default, the current date is used as a plan's status date.

How to View Task Progress

Procedure Reference:

To view task progress in an open project plan:

 On the Project Guide's Track side pane, you can also click the Check The Progress Of The Project link to display the Check Progress side pane. You can use the Status Indicator field to see if a task has been completed, is on schedule, or late.

1. Switch to Gantt Chart view.

2. Identify displayed progress elements, such as progress bars.

3. Switch to Tracking Gantt view for more detailed progress information.

4. Set status date, if desired.

5. Display progress lines, if desired.

6. Display the Variance table, if desired.

7. Compare tasks' actual start and finish dates to the tasks' baseline start and finish dates.

Progress Bars

In Gantt Chart view, tasks that have been started show progress bars. A *progress bar* is a thick black line displayed inside the task bar that shows how much of a task has been actually completed. You can modify how a progress bar is displayed by right-clicking a Gantt Chart and selecting Bar Styles from the shortcut menu.

Progress Lines

Displayed in Gantt Chart view, a *progress line* is a line drawn by Project that connects in-progress task bars. If the progress line peaks to the left, that means a task is behind schedule. If the progress line peaks to the right, the task is ahead of schedule. Progress lines can use either the current date or a status date you set. To show progress lines, right-click the Gantt Chart and select Progress Lines and click OK to show them. (Progress lines can be modified by setting a variety of options in the Progress Lines dialog box, such as showing several progress lines for different intervals if you so choose.)

ACTIVITY 2-2

Viewing Task Progress

Setup:

My CSS Week 1.mpp is open in Task Sheet view.

Scenario:

Now that you've updated the project plan with task progress data, you want to double-check the data you entered to see if tasks have been marked complete and whether or not the finish date has changed.

What You Do	How You Do It

 Use ScreenTips to help get details about each updated task.

1. **Switch back to Gantt Chart view.**

   What do you notice about tasks 1, 3, and 4 now that their progress has been updated?

   Notice the current finish date. For Task 3, after you reduced the duration from 2 days to 1, did the finish date change from the original 10/19?

   Although Gantt Chart view shows where the tasks actually are, it doesn't show where tasks should be. For that, we'll need a different view.

2. **Switch to Tracking Gantt view.**

   According to the Project Summary bar, how much progress has been made?

   According to the Research Phase Summary bar, how much progress has been made?

3. Update the project's information so the status date is *8/5/05*, and then show progress lines in the chart based on the status date.

 Use the Zoom tools as needed.

a. **Display the Project Information dialog box.**

b. **Change the Status Date to *8/5/05* and click OK.**

c. **Right-click in the chart and choose Progress lines** to display the Progress Lines dialog box.

d. If necessary, **check Always Display Current Progress Line and select At Project Status Date.**

e. **Click OK.**

4. **Is the Research Phase ahead or behind schedule?**

5. In Tracking Gantt view, **display the Variance table.**

What's the current Finish Variance for Task 2, the Research Phase summary task?

Save and close the My CSS Week 1.mpp project plan.

 The Finish Variance field is the last column in the table. Drag the Divide bar to display it.

TOPIC C

Split a Task

Up until now, our plan has been proceeding smoothly, but how often does that last? The time may come when work on a task is unavoidably interrupted for a period before it can be resumed. In this topic, you will see how to account for interruptions in your plan.

Accounting for task interruptions will help you keep your plan on track. How can you identify task interruptions in your plan? You could leave yourself a bunch of notes like, "Task 175 was interrupted for a week while the office's roof was being repaired," you could fudge the interrupted task's duration so that it doesn't impact the finish date, or you could just ignore the fact that it ever happened—to the impending doom of your project plan. The best way is to just accept the interruption by including it in your plan—which Project can help you with—and then figuring out how to accommodate it.

Split Task

A *split task* is one where the schedule is unexpectedly interrupted for a period of time. Typically, interruptions happen when there are delays in supply chains, violent weather conditions, or health issues within a project team. However, if for some reason a task's schedule is interrupted, you can split it to account for the interruption. This can be accomplished by displaying the task in Gantt Chart view and clicking the Split Task button on the Standard toolbar. By default, Project inserts a 1-day delay. If you need to increase the delay, place the mouse pointer over the right half of the split task until you see the four-headed arrow icon, and then click and drag the task to the right, until the desired date is displayed in the ScreenTip.

Remove a Split

To remove a split, place the mouse pointer over the right half of the split task until you see the four-headed arrow icon. Then just click and drag the right-most task section and drag it back until it rejoins the left task section. Keep in mind that dragging task elements in the Gantt Chart is imprecise, and that moving task bars directly affects the task's data.

How to Split a Task

Procedure Reference:

To split a task:

1. Use one of the following methods:
   - On the Standard toolbar, click the Split Task button.
   - Choose Edit→Split Task.

2. Place the mouse pointer over the task you want to split.

3. Move the mouse pointer along the task until you see the date in the ScreenTip where you want the split to occur.

4. Click the mouse button to create task sections with a 1-day split between them.

   You can split tasks multiple times.

5. Drag the right-most section to the right to increase the split, or to the left to decrease the split as needed.

ACTIVITY 2-3

Splitting a Task

Data Files:

* CSS Week 2.mpp

Setup:

Project is the active application and no project plans are open.

Scenario:

It's Monday, 8/15/05, another week has gone by, and the task progress information is trickling in from the CSS Week 2.mpp project plan's resources. The writer and staff assistant assigned to Task 5 report that, although they finished the task, they didn't finish it as scheduled. They started the 2-day task on Monday as planned, but due to the severe thunderstorm Monday night and lingering county-wide power outages, the office was closed Tuesday. Ultimately, they couldn't finish the task until Wednesday. The split task should look like Figure 2-3 when you're done.

| 4 | ✓ | 2.2 Investigate the software | Writer 1 |
| 5 | ✓ | 2.3 Search the Web | Writer 1,Staff Assistant 1 |

Figure 2-3: *Task 5 complete and split.*

What You Do	How You Do It
1. Change the current date of the CSS Week 2 project plan to *8/15/05* and mark Task 5 complete.	a. **Open CSS Week 2.mpp.**
	b. In the Project Information dialog box, **change the project's current date to** *8/15/05*
	c. **Select Task 5.**
	d. If necessary, **display the Tracking toolbar and click the 100% Complete button** to mark Task 5 as 100-percent complete.
2. **Split Task 5 so the task shows a 1-day interruption on Tuesday.**	a. With Task 5 still selected, on the Standard toolbar, **click the Split Task button** .

b. In the Gantt Chart, place the mouse pointer over the middle of Task 5's bar.

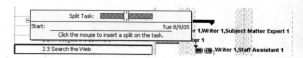

c. **Click the mouse button** to split the task into two sections.

3. **Do you have to increase or decrease the split between the sections to account for the 1-day interruption?**

_____

_____

🖈 To quickly change table views, right-click the blank gray column heading above the ID field to display a list of tables.

4. In Gantt Chart view, **display the Variance table.**

Now what's the Finish Variance for Task 2, the Research Phase summary task?

Redisplay the Entry table and save the plan as *My CSS Week 2.mpp*

Topic D

Reschedule a Task

After you split a task, it may move beyond its scheduled finish date. You can often work your project management magic to bring that task back in, so the plan doesn't slip. Sometimes, however, you may have to reschedule a task or at least a portion of it. You will learn how to do that next.

Being able to reschedule uncompleted work, although it may impact a deadline, frequently allows you to keep the scheduled resource(s) on the task in question. This ensures that the most qualified person can accomplish a mission-critical task to the best of his or her ability, without rushing the task to completion, without requiring unreasonable work hours, and without adding unqualified resources just to satisfy a deadline.

How to Reschedule a Task

Procedure Reference:

To have Project reschedule uncompleted work for a task:

1. Select the task or tasks to be rescheduled.

2. Choose Tools→Tracking→Update Project.

3. Select Reschedule Uncompleted Work To Start After and then enter the desired date.

4. Choose Selected Tasks.

5. Click OK.

6. Verify whether or not the rescheduled work has impacted the plan's finish date.

 If an uncompleted task hasn't started, it will be moved forward and given a Start No Earlier Than constraint.

Reschedule Work Button

If a project plan includes a status date, you can use the Reschedule Work button on the Tracking toolbar to quickly reschedule the remaining work of a selected task to continue from the plan's status date. (If a project plan uses the current date as its status date, clicking the Reschedule Task button will have the same effect as following the previously mentioned steps, using the Update Project dialog box.)

ACTIVITY 2-4

Rescheduling a Task's Uncompleted Work

Setup:

My CSS Week 2.mpp is open in Gantt Chart view with the Entry table displayed.

Scenario:

Continuing to update task progress, you come to Task 7. Because Task 5 was delayed, Task 7 was started a day late. The bad news continues. The writer responsible for creating the outline only accomplished 25 percent of his task before he was called away Thursday afternoon to tend to a family emergency. Rather than assign someone else to finish the task, you will need to account for the work he already did and reschedule the uncompleted work to begin again when he returns Wednesday, 8/17.

What You Do	How You Do It
1. Mark Task 7 as 25-percent complete.	a. Select Task 7.
	b. On the Tracking toolbar, **click the 25% Complete button** .
	📌 Task 7's progress bar shows that the task is 25-percent complete.
2. Reschedule the task's uncompleted work to restart after today, Tuesday, *8/16/05*.	a. If necessary, **select Task 7.**
	b. **Choose Tools→Tracking→Update Project.**
	c. If necessary, **select Reschedule Uncompleted Work To Start After and then type *8/16/05***
	d. **Select Selected Tasks.**
	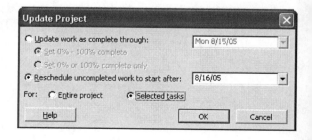
	e. **Click OK** to reschedule the task.

3. What happened when you rescheduled the uncompleted work?

4. What happened to the project plan's finish date?

TOPIC E
Filter Tasks in a Project Plan

Up to this point, we've used the Gantt Chart view to view tasks in progress, and Tracking Gantt chart view to see the project plan as a whole. That's fine if you want a big-picture view of the plan. But if you want to zoom in on just a particular type of task—milestones, for instance—you need a way to show just the relevant tasks. You will see how to do that in this topic.

Being able to view a particular type of task or resource by itself helps you separate the wheat from the chaff. For example, if you're only interested in seeing incomplete or unstarted tasks, you can have Project show you only those types of tasks, while hiding all other tasks that don't fit that criteria. This allows you to isolate the problems so you can take the appropriate and suitable action, if necessary.

Filters

Definition:

Project's *Filter* tool on the Formatting toolbar includes several selection criteria that allows you to include (or exclude) specific data in a view. You can use this to apply a variety of filters quickly.

Example:

Which filters are available is determined by the type of view. Some common task filters include Critical, Incomplete Tasks, and Slipping Tasks. Some common resource filters include Slipping Assignments, Work Incomplete, and Work Overbudget. If you want to just highlight data that meets a filter's criteria so that it can be viewed within the context of all data, you can display the More Filters dialog box (choose Project→ Filtered For:All Tasks→More Filters), select a filter and click the Highlight button (see Figure 2-4).

 For a comprehensive filter list, enter "Available Filters" in the Ask A Question box on the Standard toolbar.

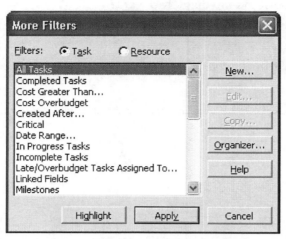

Figure 2-4: *The More Filters dialog box.*

AutoFilters

If you want to filter table data quickly within a field, you can use *AutoFilters* either by clicking the AutoFilter button 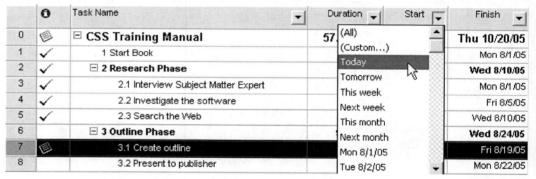 on the Formatting toolbar or by choosing Project→

Filtered For→AutoFilter. This places a field-specific, drop-down list of AutoFilters to the right of each column heading (see Figure 2-5). For example, if you wanted to see tasks scheduled to begin today, you could click the AutoFilter button and select the Today value from the Start column's AutoFilter list. Any tasks scheduled to start on the current date will be displayed. To turn off AutoFilters, click the AutoFilter button again.

Figure 2-5: *An AutoFilter list.*

How to Filter Tasks in a Project Plan

Procedure Reference:

To filter tasks in a project plan:

1. If necessary, switch to the view in which you want the filtered results to be displayed.

    ⚠ Switching views after a filter has been applied removes the filter.

2. Select the desired filter using one of the following methods:

    • On the Formatting toolbar, display the Filter drop-down list and select a filter.

- Choose Project→Filtered For and choose a filter.

 To see all available filters, select the More Filters option.

Remove a Filter

To remove a task filter and display all tasks again, select All Tasks from either the Filter drop-down list on the Formatting toolbar or from the Project→Filtered For menu. To remove a resource filter, select All Resources using one of the aforementioned methods. You can also switch views to remove a filter.

ACTIVITY 2-5

Filtering a Project Plan to Display Slipping Tasks

Setup:

My CSS Week 2.mpp is open in Gantt Chart view and the remaining work for Task 7 has been rescheduled.

Scenario:

Now that Task 7 has been rescheduled, you wonder what other tasks in your plan have been affected. The best way to see the rescheduling effect is to filter the project plan's tasks to show only those uncompleted tasks that have been delayed as a result of Task 7.

What You Do	How You Do It
1. **Apply the Slipping Tasks filter to the plan.**	a. On the Formatting toolbar, on the Toolbar Options button, **display the Filter drop-down list.**
	b. **Scroll down and select Slipping Tasks** to apply the filter to the plan.

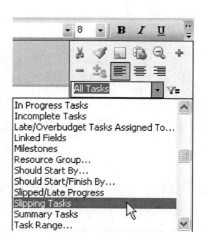

In the Filter drop-down list, you can type the letter "s" to jump quickly to the filters that begin with "s."

2. **How many of the remaining tasks have slipped as a result of rescheduling Task 7?**

3. **Besides applying a filter, such as Slipping Tasks, what other ways could you use Project to check to see what tasks are behind schedule?**

4. **Remove the Slipping Tasks filter and save the plan.**	a. From the Filter drop-down list, **select All Tasks.**
	b. **Save the project plan file.**

PRACTICE ACTIVITY 2-6

Filtering for Tasks on the Critical Path

Activity Time:

5 minutes

Scenario:

Now that you've identified the slipping tasks, you want to see which of those are on the critical path. This information will also help you decide what steps to take, if any, to adjust the plan.

 Don't forget to remove all filters before continuing.

1. **Filter the project plan so that only tasks on the critical path are displayed.**

2. **Which of the remaining tasks are on the critical path?**

3. **Remove the Critical filter so all tasks are displayed.**

TOPIC F

Save an Interim Project Plan

With the project plan underway and task progress, or lack thereof, affecting the baseline's initial start and finish dates, you need to make a decision as to whether or not to try to adjust slipping tasks to meet the original baseline dates, or record the new start dates as part of your project plan and go from there. This topic will show you how to save the new dates as an interim project plan.

By recording new start/finish dates, you can effectively track progress at various stages in your plan. (You can also compare these stages to the original baseline.) This way, you can more accurately monitor costs, resources, and task progress at specific points, based upon the project plan's most current updates. For example, if one of your suppliers can't deliver raw materials until a week later than scheduled in the baseline plan, all of the plan's information will be displayed as a week late. However, if you take this delay into account and create a new set of start and finish dates from that point on, the new dates let you confidently report to your stakeholders that—after that delay—the plan is still on schedule.

Interim Plan

Separate from a project plan's baseline dates, an *interim plan* is a saved set of current start and finish dates for tasks after a plan has begun. Project can accommodate up to 10 interim plans, and each one can be used to signify a particular stage or phase of a project plan. Interim plans can help you compare a plan's current progress ("Where are we now?") to its scheduled baseline dates, "Where should we be?" However, unlike a baseline plan—which saves original data for costs, dates, durations, and work—an interim plan only saves start and finish dates.

How to Save an Interim Project Plan

Procedure Reference:

To save current start and finish dates into the first interim project plan:

1. Choose Tools→Tracking→Save Baseline.

2. Select Save Interim Plan.

3. Click OK.

Clear Interim Plans

If you ever need to clear saved interim plans from a project plan, it's done in the Clear Baseline dialog box (choose Tools→Tracking→Clear Baseline). You might need to clear interim plans occasionally if your project plan has a lengthy duration.

ACTIVITY 2-7

Setting an Interim Plan

Setup:

My CSS Week 2.mpp is open in Gantt Chart view and all filters have been removed.

Scenario:

Once you have your tasks updated in your My CSS Week 2 project plan, you know things have slipped. The publisher clearly stated to you that he wants to know when the plan gets behind schedule, and by how much. He also has asked you to somehow mark each point in the project plan where there have been delays, so that the delays can be discussed at the status meetings.

What You Do	How You Do It
1. Display the statistics for My CSS Week 2.mpp. (Choose Project→Project Information and click Statistics.)	
How far has the Finish date slipped?	
Close the Project Statistics dialog box.	

2. Save an interim plan.

    a. **Choose Tools→Tracking→Save Baseline.**

    b. **Select Save Interim Plan, leaving the default options selected.**

    c. **Verify that Entire Project is selected.**

    d. **Click OK** to create the new interim plan.

TOPIC G
Create a Custom Table

You've experienced adding information to a project plan and you know that a plan can contain literally thousands of data items. Project's default tables go a long way toward providing you with meaningful ways to display that data. But the occasion may arise when you want to see information that may not be available in a default table. In this topic, you will see how to create your own tables.

Creating a custom table gives you a way to display the data you want, where you want, without the distraction of other unnecessary columns of data. You can display all of the data you want in one place, which means no more switching back and forth between views, using scraps of paper to jot down the information you want to compare. It also means that you can display those pieces of data in your project plan whenever you want. You needn't create the table over and over. Build your table one time to display your data every time.

How to Create a Custom Table

Procedure Reference:

You can create custom resource or task tables by either starting with a new blank table, which can be a lot of unnecessary work, or by copying an existing table that contains fields you want to use in your custom table. The steps are essentially the same, regardless of the method you prefer.

To create a custom table based on an existing table:

1. Display the More Tables dialog box.

2. Select the existing task or resource table you want to base your custom table on and click Copy.

3. Give the new table a unique name and check Show In Menu if you want it to appear on the View→Table submenu.

4. Cut, copy, paste, insert, or delete table rows, as needed.

> When you're creating a custom table, don't be confused by the layout of the Table Definition dialog box. The rows actually become columns when displayed in the table.

5. Format the rows, as needed.

6. Apply the new table.

Edit Custom Tables

Once you create a custom table, you can edit it whenever you want by selecting the table in the More Tables dialog box and clicking Edit. The steps for editing the table are identical to those when you created it.

ACTIVITY 2-8

Creating a Custom Table to Compare Baseline and Interim Start/Finish Data

Setup:

My CSS Week 2.mpp is open in Gantt Chart view and the interim baseline has been saved.

Scenario:

For your My CSS Week 2 project plan, you've set an interim plan for the sake of being able to compare this data to the baseline start and finish dates. You've looked over Project's default tables to see if there's one that would allow you to do this, but the closest you came was the Baseline table. Unfortunately, it doesn't contain the interim plan information, but you can use it as your starting point. When you're done and have applied the table, it should look similar to Figure 2-6.

	Task Name	Baseline Start	Baseline Finish	Interim Start 1	Interim Finish 1
0	⊟ CSS Training Manua	Mon 8/1/05 ▾	Wed 10/19/05	Mon 8/1/05	Thu 10/20/05
1	1 Start Book	Mon 8/1/05	Mon 8/1/05	Mon 8/1/05	Mon 8/1/05
2	⊟ 2 Research Phase	Mon 8/1/05	Wed 8/10/05	Mon 8/1/05	Wed 8/10/05
3	2.1 Interview Subje	Mon 8/1/05	Tue 8/2/05	Mon 8/1/05	Mon 8/1/05
4	2.2 Investigate the	Wed 8/3/05	Mon 8/8/05	Tue 8/2/05	Fri 8/5/05
5	2.3 Search the We	Tue 8/9/05	Wed 8/10/05	Mon 8/8/05	Wed 8/10/05

Figure 2-6: *The custom BASELINE/INTERIM DATES table.*

What You Do	How You Do It
1. **Make a copy of the Baseline task table.**	a. **Choose View→Table:Entry→More Tables** to display the More Tables dialog box.
	b. Next to the Tables option, **verify that Task is selected.**

c. From the Tables list box, **select Baseline.**

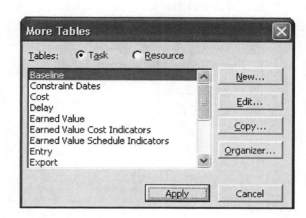

d. **Click Copy** to display the Table Definition dialog box.

2. **Name the table *BASELINE/INTERIM DATES*, mark it so that it will be displayed in the View→Table menu, and remove the Baseline Duration, Baseline Work, and Baseline Cost rows.**

    It's a good idea to use all capital letters to name any project plan items that you create, to easily distinguish between custom elements and those that came with the application.

a. In the Name text box, **type *BASELINE/ INTERIM DATES***

b. **Check Show In Menu.**

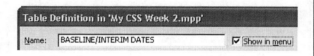

c. In the Field Name column, **select Baseline Duration.**

d. **Click Delete Row.**

e. **Delete the Baseline Work and Baseline Cost rows.** The ID, Name, Baseline Start, and Baseline Finish rows remain.

3. Add a new row for the interim plan's Start1 field, giving it a title of *Interim Start 1* and add a new row for the interim plan's Finish1 field, with a title of *Interim Finish 1*. Then, apply your custom table.

a. In the row below the Baseline Finish field name, from the Field Name drop-down list, **select Start1 and press Enter.**

b. In the Start1 row, **select the Title field, type *Interim Start 1* and press Enter.**

c. Below the Start1 field name, from the Field Name drop-down list, **select Finish1 and press Enter.**

d. In the Finish1 row, **name the Title field *Interim Finish 1* and press Enter.**

e. **Click OK** to create the custom table.

f. If necessary, from the More Tables dialog box, **select BASELINE/INTERIM DATES.**

g. **Click Apply** to apply your custom table to the Gantt Chart view.

> If necessary, adjust the Divide bar and column widths so that you can see the table's column headings and data.

4. Using the CSS Training Manual project summary task, Task 0, what's the difference between the project's Baseline Finish date and the Interim Finish 1 date?

5. Comparing the Baseline Finish date and the Interim Finish 1 date for task summaries, during which phase did the plan slip?

Topic H

Add Custom Columns to a Table

Tables are great for showing Project's default columns of information. But when Project fails to supply you with a column in which you can record and display custom data, you need to take it upon yourself to create your own custom column. This topic will show you how.

Creating a custom column lets you capture and display exactly the information you want without being limited by Project's default offerings. What if you need to include a column to enter and display the name of ancillary products produced by a manufacturing task? You can bet that Project doesn't offer you a column named "Ancillary Products." You could type these product names in the task's notes, but the information wouldn't display by default, so it may be overlooked. Making a custom table to accommodate the custom data is by far a better solution; the column makes it easy to enter the data, as well as display it.

How to Add Custom Columns to a Table

Procedure Reference:

To create a custom column, or field, to be displayed in a table:

1. Choose Tools→Customize→Fields.

2. Select the type of table you want the custom field displayed in (either Task or Resource).

3. Select the type of field.

4. Select the actual field you want to customize.

5. Rename the field.

6. Customize the field, as desired.

7. Click OK to create the field.

8. In the desired table, right-click a column heading and select Insert Column.

9. Select the field name you want to display and then format it, if desired.

10. Click OK to insert the column.

Custom Field Types

The formatting and the type of the data you want to capture will determine which type of custom field you select. (See Figure 2-7.) Project provides you with Cost (currency), Date, Duration, Finish, Flag (yes or no), Number, Outline Code, Start, and Text fields. For example, if you want a field to contain textual information, you would create a custom Text field.

 If you use Project Professional's Enterprise features, there are separate Enterprise fields that can be customized.

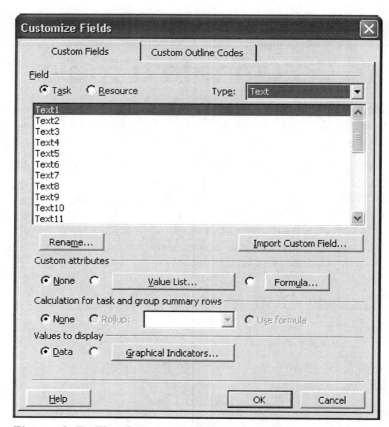

Figure 2-7: *The Customize Fields dialog box.*

Show/Hide Columns

In tables, columns are inserted to the left of the selected column. To insert a custom column, or field, display the table in which you want to contain the column. Then right-click the desired column heading and select Insert Column. Select your custom field from the list and click OK. If you choose to hide a column, you can right-click the column you want to hide and select Hide Column from the shortcut menu.

ACTIVITY 2-9

Adding a Custom Field to a Table

Setup:

The My CSS Week 2.mpp plan is open in Gantt Chart view, with the custom BASELINE/ INTERIM DATES table displayed.

Scenario:

Your sponsor has asked that you keep track of any documents, such as the CSS Outline, that have to be delivered to stakeholders for the CSS project plan. She wants the names of the deliverables to be displayed in a column in the Entry table so that the field can be conveniently monitored and updated. When you are done, your custom field should look like Figure 2-8.

	ⓘ	Deliverables	Task Name
0	📖		⊟ CSS Training Manual
1	✓		1 Start Book
2	✓		⊟ 2 Research Phase
3	✓		2.1 Interview Subject Matter Expert
4	✓		2.2 Investigate the software
5	✓		2.3 Search the Web
6			⊟ 3 Outline Phase
7	📖	CSS Outline.doc	3.1 Create outline

Figure 2-8: *The custom Deliverables field.*

What You Do	How You Do It
1. **Create a Text type task field named** *Deliverables*.	a. **Choose Tools→Customize→Fields.**
	b. If necessary, in the Field area, **select Task.**
	c. From the Type drop-down list, **select Text.**
	d. **Verify that Text1 is selected in the Field list.**
	e. **Click Rename.**
	f. **Type** *Deliverables* **and click OK.**
	g. **Click OK again** to create the new Deliverables field and to close the Customize Fields dialog box.

2. In the Entry table, **insert the Deliverables column to the left of the Task Name column.**

    a. **Display the Entry table.**

    b. **Right-click the Task Name column heading and select Insert Column** to display the Column Definition dialog box.

    c. From the Field Name drop-down list, **select Deliverables (Text1).**

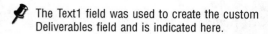 The Text1 field was used to create the custom Deliverables field and is indicated here.

    d. **Click OK** to insert the column displaying the custom Deliverables field.

3. In the Deliverables field for Task 7, enter *CSS Outline.doc*.

    a. **Select the Deliverables field for Task 7.**

    b. **Type *CSS Outline.doc* and press Enter.**

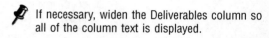 If necessary, widen the Deliverables column so all of the column text is displayed.

TOPIC I

Hyperlink Documents to Tasks

You may need to open supporting files to accomplish certain tasks throughout the course of working with a project plan. Project allows you to connect such files to a project plan using hyperlinks. This topic will show you how to do that.

In Project, hyperlinks provide anyone who has access to the project plan with the ability to open planning documents, such as statements of work, or applicable Web pages, without having to waste time searching local disk drives or the Internet. Such one-click convenience can make a task easier. For example, if a task requires a resource to fill out a supply requisition form, you can provide a link to that form right in the task. You can even create a hyperlink between two tasks.

Hyperlinks

A *hyperlink* is text that contains an interactive link that, when clicked, displays a location in a project plan, a file in its own application, or a Web page in a browser. Typically, hyperlinks are used to keep the file size of a project plan to a minimum. Rather than embedding a file within a project plan, which can quickly bloat a plan's file size, a hyperlink merely stores the location of a file. A hyperlink can be attached to any task, resource, or assignment, and is typically displayed in the Indicators column as a hyperlink icon. Hyperlinks to Web addresses can also be typed directly in the Notes tab of a task, resource, or assignment's Information dialog box.

How to Hyperlink Documents to Tasks

Procedure Reference:

To hyperlink any file or Web page to a project plan:

1. Select a view, task, resource, or assignment where the hyperlink will be located.

2. Choose one of the following methods:
   - On the Standard toolbar, click the Insert Hyperlink button.
   - Right-click the desired item and choose Hyperlink from the shortcut menu.
   - Choose Insert→Hyperlink.
   - Press Ctrl+K.

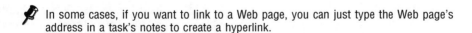 In some cases, if you want to link to a Web page, you can just type the Web page's address in a task's notes to create a hyperlink.

3. If desired, enter the text you want to be displayed when the mouse pointer is positioned over the hyperlink icon in the Indicators column.

4. Select the Existing File Or Web Page Link To option.

5. Browse for the file or Web page to which you want to hyperlink.

6. Click OK to insert the hyperlink.

7. Test the hyperlink.

Hyperlink Modification

If you make a mistake creating a hyperlink, or if a hyperlink no longer serves a purpose, you can either edit it or remove it entirely. Just right-click the hyperlink icon in the Indicators column and select the applicable option from the Hyperlink choice on the shortcut menu.

ACTIVITY 2-10

Hyperlinking a Word Document to a Task

Data Files:

- CSS Outline.doc

Setup:

My CSS Week 2.mpp plan is open in Gantt Chart view, and CSS Outline.doc has been entered in the Deliverables column for Task 7.

Scenario:

The Marketing department is notorious for asking "quick questions" that often require you to hunt down and open the training manual's outline, CSS Outline, which contains the answers. To help you address this inevitable situation, you decide to hyperlink the outline document to Task 7.

What You Do	How You Do It
1. Create a hyperlink from Task 7 to CSS Outline.doc.	a. If necessary, **select Task 7.**
	b. On the Standard toolbar, **click the More Options button and then click the Insert Hyperlink button** 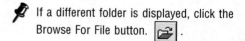 .
	c. If necessary, **select the Existing File Or Web Page option.**
	✏ If you are using the Standard version of Project 2003, select the Existing File Or Web Page option.
	d. If necessary, from the Look In drop-down list, **select My Documents.**
	✏ If a different folder is displayed, click the Browse For File button.
	e. From the file list, **select CSS Outline.doc.** Because nothing was entered in the Text To Display text box, the selected file's name is entered there automatically.
	f. **Click OK.**

2. **What do you notice about Task 7?**

---

3. **Test the hyperlink and then exit Word.**

   ⚠️ If the hyperlink doesn't work as expected, remove it and try applying it again. (Right-click the hyperlink icon in the Indicators column and choose Hyperlink→ Remove Hyperlink.)

   a. In the Indicators column for Task 7, **click the hyperlink icon.**

   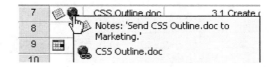

   b. If a message box is displayed asking if you want to continue, **click Yes.**

   c. **Verify that CSS Outline.doc opens in Word.**

   d. **Exit Word without saving changes,** if prompted.

---

4. **How might you use hyperlinks in your projects?**

   Save My CSS Week 2.mpp and close the project plan file.

Lesson 2 Follow-up

Nice job! You have just covered the basic skills for updating a project plan—skills necessary for successfully delivering your plan on time. You can now enter and view task progress. You can filter, reschedule, and split tasks as needed. In addition to updating task information, you can make your own tables either to display project plan information you want or to create a hyperlink to project-related information so that it's displayed in its own application when the link is clicked. You're now ready to share the plan's progress with stakeholders and team members.

1. **What consequences might there be if a plan is not updated regularly during the project? Discuss your answers with the class.**

2. Have you ever been on a project that was very well managed from start to finish? Have you ever been on one that wasn't? Describe your experiences to the class about either situation.

LESSON 3
Creating Custom Reports

Lesson Objectives:

In this lesson, you will create custom reports.

You will:

*   Create a custom report.
*   Modify a custom report's header and footer.
*   Add a picture to a custom report.
*   Modify a custom report's margins.
*   Print a custom report.

Introduction

During a project plan's life cycle, collecting and inputting task progress is only part of the job. Perhaps more significant is the need to disseminate this information in a meaningful way. After all, what good does having all this information do if it doesn't get to the people who need it? In this lesson, you will see how Project provides a variety of options to accomplish this.

Customizing project plan information allows you to provide project members with timely and targeted information applicable to them. For instance, a project's line worker probably doesn't need to know about a report's cash flow numbers, nor would a project's sponsor be likely to care much about a report detailing resource workload. Generating a custom report with need-to-know information for each audience saves them time, because they don't have to sift through pages of details that have no direct impact on fulfilling their project role. Being able to create customized reports that meet the requirements of a particular audience helps keep the communication channels open and information flowing properly in a consistent and efficient manner.

TOPIC A

Create a Custom Report

You've created a custom table to capture information unique to Project, so that you can view it on your screen. That's fine for you, but what if others want to see that information? In this topic, you will provide that information to others using the most convenient method possible, a custom report.

A custom report allows you to display information in a "formal," legible, and easily repeated manner, so that it can be included either in the regular status report or printed on demand as a stand-alone piece. You could print a view that includes the desired information, but that can involve adjusting Zoom levels, column widths, and other items—wasting time and paper on a lot of trial and error. For larger projects with hundreds or thousands of tasks, printing a view may be difficult to manage and still be able to get readable results. Creating a custom report ensures that your results will appear consistent every time.

How to Create a Custom Report

Procedure Reference:

To create a custom report:

1. Choose View→Reports.

2. Select Custom and click Select.

3. Create your custom report using one of the following methods:
    - From scratch—Click New, select a report type (Task, Resource, Monthly Calendar, or Crosstab), and click OK.
    - From an existing report—Select the existing report on which you want to base your custom report and click Copy.

4. Define the report elements (name, period, table, and any applicable filters), add details, and any desired sorting options, and then click OK.

5. Preview and edit the new report as needed.

ACTIVITY 3-1

Creating a Custom Report from a Custom Table

Data Files:

*   CSS Week 12.mpp

Scenario:

It's Monday, 10/17/05. Week 12 of the CSS project plan is now complete and, with only 1 week to go, all task progress information is current. However, after the scheduling difficulties back in week 2, one of the project sponsors is still a little nervous about meeting the 10/19 finish date—even though you've told her that you were able to get the plan back on track and that everything has gone smoothly since. To help alleviate the sponsor's concern, you decide to create a new task report based on the custom FINISH DATES table for her.

What You Do	How You Do It
1. Open CSS Week 12.mpp and set the current date to *10/17/05*. In the CSS Week 12 project plan, **display the custom FINISH DATES table so you can see all of its fields.** **What columns of information are displayed?**	
2. Begin creating a new task report.	a. **Choose View→Reports.** b. **Select the Custom option.**  Custom... **Click Select** to display the Custom Reports dialog box. c. **Click New** to display the Define New Report dialog box.

d.   If necessary, in the Report Type list box, **select Task.**

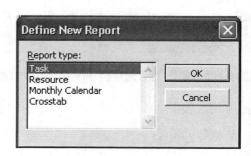

Click OK to begin defining the new task report.

3.   **Name the new task report** *FINISH DATES REPORT* **and make sure it reflects all task information from the FINISH DATES table over the course of the entire project.**

a.   In the Name text box, **type** *FINISH DATES REPORT*

b.   If necessary, from the Period drop-down list, **select Entire Project.**

c.   From the Table drop-down list, **select FINISH DATES.**

d.   **Verify that All Tasks is displayed in the Filter drop-down list box.**

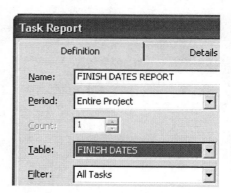

e.   **Click OK** to create the new report and to return to the Custom Reports dialog box.

4. Preview the FINISH DATES REPORT.

   Are all the columns of information displayed on the first page of the report?

   🖉 Use the Zoom and the Multiple Pages buttons as needed.

5. What other information is displayed at the top and bottom of the report pages?

6. Close the Preview window and all open dialog boxes and save the plan as *My CSS Week 12.mpp*.	a. Close the report's Preview window.
	b. Close the Custom Reports dialog box.
	c. Close the Reports dialog box.
	d. Save the plan as *My CSS Week 12.mpp*

TOPIC B

Modify a Custom Report's Header and Footer

When you create custom reports, they retain many default settings. The information displayed at the top and bottom of the page, for instance, is part of these default settings. That information is a start, but those items may provide enough information for your report. It's time to take a look at those areas and see how you can change that information to suit the needs of your audience.

In a report, the information printed at the top and bottom of each page—a publication title, author and/or company name, page numbers, and so on, provides context for your audience. How many times have you gone to a meeting and were given a handout of some kind that didn't have any of this identifying information along the page's margins? You pick the pages up two weeks later and you have to strain your brain trying to recall where and when you received it and who gave it to you. Why put your audience through this memory test? Whether you place this concise and descriptive identifying information at the top of the page or bottom, you can use it to provide readers with immediate context and set the stage for the real star of the show—the data printed between the top and bottom margins.

Headers and Footers

In Project, a *header* contains information that appears at the top of every printed view or report page, and a *footer* contains information that appears at the bottom of every printed view or report page. Each view and report can have its own header and footer. Typically, headers and footers make your printouts more appealing and more useful to your target audience—stakeholders and team members—by including details like your company name, dates, page numbers, and so on. Headers and footers each have three Alignment tabs: left, right, and center. (See Figure 3-1.) And each alignment region can contain different information. Headers can contain up to five lines of information, whereas footers can contain up to three lines.

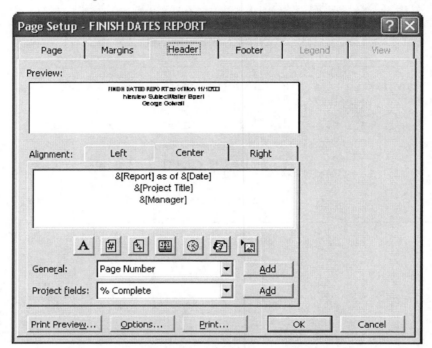

Figure 3-1: *The Header tab in a report's Page Setup dialog box.*

The Legend and View tabs are only available when modifying the page setup for a view.

General and Project Fields

Besides being able to just type your own text into header and footer areas of the Page Setup dialog box, Project lets you automatically add general project plan information values from the file's Project Information and Properties dialog boxes, as well as specific Project fields taken directly from the plan itself. Adding these values to headers and footers can save you some typing, and if the values ever change in the project plan, they are automatically updated in the header and footer. The added values are represented in the Alignment tab by an ampersand (&) followed by the value name in brackets. (See Figure 3-1.) For instance, the value for Company Name is &[Company]. Some common General values include Page Number, Project Title, Manager Name, and so on. Common Project Field values include Cost Variance, Duration, and custom fields.

Format Text Font

In the Page Setup dialog box, you can modify font attributes of the text displayed in headers and footers by clicking the Format Text Font button $\boxed{\text{A}}$. You can change the text's font, style, size, and color, as well as see a sample of your changes before you apply them. Note that each alignment region can contain different text formatting.

How to Modify a Custom Report's Header and Footer

Procedure Reference:

To modify a custom report's header and footer:

1. Display the Custom Reports dialog box.

2. Select the Report you want to customize.

3. Click Setup to display the Page Setup dialog box.

4. Select the Header tab.

5. Remove any unwanted default fields.

6. Add the information you want to the Left, Center, and Right Alignment tabs, as needed.

7. Select the Footer tab and repeat steps 5 and 6, as desired.

8. Click OK.

9. Preview your modifications, as desired.

Page Setup Options for a View

You have a couple additional Page Setup tabs when setting up a view. The first tab, Legends, can only be viewed and modified when modifying the page setup for the Calendar, Gantt Chart, or Network Diagram views. You can format a legend very much in the same way you can modify a header and footer; however, you can also choose whether or not to print the legend on every page, a separate page, or not at all. The View tab lets you set view-specific options, such as whether or not to print all sheet columns, notes, blank pages, and totals on each page. To modify Page Setup options for a view, choose either File→Page Setup or View→Header And Footer.

ACTIVITY 3-2

Modifying the Finish Dates Report's Header and Footer

Setup:

My CSS Week 12 is open in Gantt Chart view with the custom FINISH DATES table displayed.

Scenario:

You created the FINISH DATES REPORT for Carol Pennelo, the anxious project sponsor. However, you need to modify the information in the header and footer, as shown in Figure 3-2.

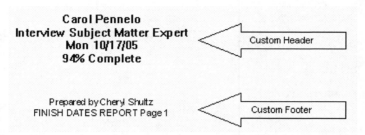

Figure 3-2: *Preview of the custom header and footer for the FINISH DATES REPORT.*

What You Do	How You Do It
1. For the custom FINISH DATES REPORT, **replace the default header information with who the report is intended for, the project title, the project's current date, and the percent complete.**	a. **Display the Custom Reports dialog box.** (Choose View→Reports and double-click Custom.)
	b. **Select the FINISH DATES REPORT.**
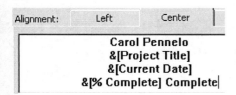	c. **Click Setup** to display the report's Page Setup dialog box.

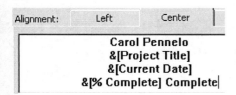

Alignment: | Left | Center |

Carol Pennelo
&[Project Title]
&[Current Date]
&[% Complete] Complete

 Notice that the Legend and View tabs are grayed out in the Page Setup dialog box. They are unavailable when setting up a report's pages.

d. **Select the Header tab.**

e. If necessary, **display the Center alignment tab.**

f. In the Center tab's text box, **select and delete all of the default information.**

 You may need to put the insertion point in the text box after you delete the information.

g. In the Center alignment area, **type** *Carol Pennelo* **and press Enter.**

h. From the General drop-down list, **select Project Title.**

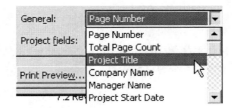

General: Page Number

Page Number
Total Page Count
Project Title
Company Name
Manager Name
Project Start Date

Project fields:

Print Preview...

Click Add, and press Enter.

i. Again, from the General drop-down list, **select Project Current Date, click Add, and press Enter.**

j. If necessary, from the Project Fields drop-down list, **select % Complete and click Add.**

k. After the % Complete value in the text box, **type the word** *Complete*.

2. In the Footer area, **include your name as the person who prepared the report and the report's name before the page number value that's already there.**

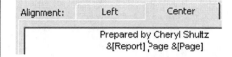

a. **Select the Footer tab and verify that the Center alignment tab is selected.**

b. **Place the insertion point before the word "Page."**

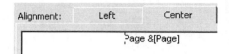

c. **Type** *Prepared by*, **press Spacebar, and then type your name and press Enter.**

> If you are listed as the project plan's manager in the file's Properties dialog box, you can add the Manager Name value from the General drop-down list.

d. From the General drop-down list, **add Report Name.**

e. **Click OK** to accept the changes and return to the Custom Reports dialog box.

3. **Preview the FINISH DATES REPORT.**

Does the header and footer information you entered look like you expected it to? If not, discuss your expectations with the class. How might you change the information to be displayed as you want it?

What other information might you include in the Header and Footer areas? Discuss your ideas with the class.

Is the Finish Variance column still on the second page of the report?

Close the Preview window, leaving the Custom Reports dialog box open.

TOPIC C

Add a Picture to a Report

With descriptive text in your custom report's headers and footers, you've already provided a significant amount of contextual information. But have you provided enough? Does the report stand out? Or does it look like every other report you've seen? In this topic, you will see how adding a picture is yet another way to enhance your custom report.

Whether at home or at the office, we are often inundated with landslides of reading material. Often we will choose which piece to read simply by picking up the first one that seems to catch your eye. Part of this attraction is a document's graphical appeal. By including a picture in a report, you not only add visual interest, but you can also increase a report's usefulness. For instance, adding a picture of a palm tree can instantly help a reader to recall that the report was passed out at your company's winter meetings in Palm Springs. In short, adding a picture to your custom reports can make your information more identifiable, as well as appear more attractive and professional.

How to Add a Picture to a Report

Procedure Reference:

If you want a picture displayed in a view or custom report, you need to put it in either the Header or Footer area. To add a picture to a custom report's header or footer:

1. Choose View→Reports and double-click the Custom option.

    To modify a default report's header or footer, choose the report you want and click Select. Then, click the Page Setup button in the Preview window.

2. Select the custom report in the Reports list box and click Setup.

3. Display the custom report's desired header or footer.

4. Select the Alignment tab where you want the picture to be displayed.

5. Click the Insert Picture button.

6. Locate the picture you want to include, select it, and click Insert.

7. Resize the picture, as needed.

8. Preview the custom report, as needed.

Graphics Areas

Headers and footers aren't the only place you can insert or paste pictures. You can add several different picture file formats, charts, and drawings to other graphics areas in a project plan as well. A *graphics area* is any place in Project where a graphic element can be inserted, like notes, legends, and Gantt Charts. By being able to add graphics to so many places makes it relatively easy to enhance any project plan with visuals.

Picture Modifications

Once a picture has been inserted into a header or footer, you can make some small modifications to it. An inserted picture can be resized by dragging any of the file's selection handles. The picture can also be moved around within a header or footer's Alignment tab. If you want to remove a picture after it has been inserted, simply select it in the Alignment tab and press Delete.

ACTIVITY 3-3

Inserting a Picture into a Custom Report's Footer

Data Files:

*   CPLogo.jpg

Setup:

The My CSS Week 12.mpp file is open and the Custom Reports dialog box is displayed.

Scenario:

After previewing the Header and Footer areas of the FINISH DATES REPORT, you realize that you don't have any indication that the report has been created by Coleman Publishing. Rather than enter the company name in the header or footer, you decide to add the company logo to the report.

What You Do	How You Do It
1. For the FINISH DATES REPORT, **insert the company logo in the footer's Right alignment tab.** If you closed the Custom Reports dialog box, choose View→Reports, select Custom, and click Select.	a. If necessary, in the Custom Reports list box, **select the FINISH DATES REPORT.** b. **Click Setup.** c. If necessary, **select the Footer tab.** d. **Select the Right alignment tab.** e. **Click the Insert Picture button** . f. If necessary, from the Look In drop-down list, **select My Documents.** g. **Select CPLogo.jpg.**

h. **Click Insert** to add the black-and-white picture of the person reading a book.

2. **Use Print Preview to display the report's footer.**

   Which preview do you find more useful? The Page Setup dialog box's Preview area or the Preview window? Why?

   Close the Preview window, leaving the Custom Reports dialog box open.

Topic D
Modify a Custom Report's Margins

Once your headers and footers are complete, it's time to make sure that all of the data you want to show is clearly displayed in your report. After all, what's the point of providing a report if it doesn't display the information the way that it's intended to? In this topic, you will see how to modify page margins to best present the report's data.

Modifying margins gives you a way to control how much whitespace is displayed around the top, bottom, left, and right edges of the pages in your custom report. Why would you want to change the default margin settings? Perhaps you plan to print your document on company letterhead or stationery, which would require a wider top margin. What if you need to squeeze a bit more text on the page? You could reduce the margins to accommodate more data. Or, what if you want to make wider margins to provide people with room to jot down notes? So they can do this, you could expand the right margin.

How to Modify a Custom Report's Margins

Procedure Reference:

To modify a custom report's margins, the whitespace on all four sides of a page:

1. Choose View→Reports and double-click the Custom option.

   To modify a default report's margins, display the report you want in the Preview window. Next, click the Page Setup button to access the Margin settings.

   To modify margins for a view, choose File→Page Setup and select the Margins tab.

2. Select the custom report in the Reports list box and click Setup.

3. Select the Margins tab.

4. Use the spin boxes to increase or decrease the Top, Right, Bottom, and Left margin settings.

   Your printer determines how near data can be printed to the edge of a page.

5. Preview the custom report or view, as needed.

ACTIVITY 3-4

Modifying a Custom Report's Margins

Setup:

The My CSS Week 12.mpp file is open, the Preview window is closed, and the Custom Reports dialog box is displayed.

Scenario:

With the header and footer information updated, you realize that you still need to get the Finish Variance column on the first page of the report. Modifying the Left and Right margins should do the trick.

LESSON 3

What You Do	How You Do It

1. For the custom FINISH DATES REPORT, **adjust the left and right margins so the Finish Variance column is displayed on the first page of the report.**

 To display the Finish Variance column on the first page, the amount by which you adjust the margins may vary slightly from the measurements below, depending upon the printer driver installed on your computer.

 If you closed the Custom Reports dialog box, choose View→Reports, select Custom, and click Select.

a. If necessary, in the Custom Reports list box, **select FINISH DATES REPORT.**

b. **Click Setup.**

c. **Select the Margins tab.**

 In the Preview window, you can use the Page Setup button to return to the Margins tab quickly.

d. **Decrease the Left margin from 0.75 inches to 0.5 inches.**

e. **Decrease the Right margin from 0.75 inches to 0.5 inches.**

2. **Click Print Preview.**

Is the Finish Variance column now on the report's first page?

What other methods might you try to get more information on a printed page?

PRACTICE ACTIVITY 3-5

Modifying a Custom Report's Top Margin

Activity Time:

5 minutes

Setup:

The My CSS Week 12.mpp file is open in the Preview window.

Scenario:

Since the project plan began, Carol Pennelo has been telling you how she has been keeping a three-ring binder of all the project plan information you've been supplying. However, if Carol punches three holes in the top of the report, she will punch holes right through the header.

 Use the Page Setup button in the Preview window.

1. **Display the Margins tab for the FINISH DATES REPORT.**

2. **Increase the top margin so that a three-ring hole punch won't put holes through the report's header. Another inch should be sufficient.**

3. **What happened to the report information after you increased the top margin?**

4. **Close the Preview window, leaving the Custom Reports dialog box open.**

TOPIC E

Print a Custom Report

Your custom report is all set for printing. Think of all that you've done to get it where it is now! In this topic, you will see the steps you need to take to print your report.

A printed report is a tangible, easily stored record of project events that can be referred to at any time. This paper reflection of everyone's hard work is a great way to provide clear details in an easily interpreted format.

Print Options

Project provides you with a variety of printing options. However, if you want to change a print option, you will need to display the Print dialog box. There you can modify a variety of options: Printer Properties, Print Range, Copies, Timescale, and Manual Page Breaks. Available options are determined by the type of report or view being printed. The Timescale option, as shown in Figure 3-3, is only available when a report includes assignment, resource, or task details that are distributed over a given time period. However, if you just want a quick print out of a view without modifying any options, you can just use the Print button 🖨 on the Standard toolbar or you can display the Print dialog box and just click OK.

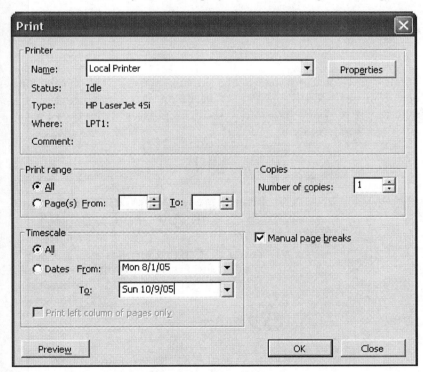

Figure 3-3: *Available printing options.*

How to Print a Custom Report

Procedure Reference:

To print a custom report,

1. Select the custom report you want to print in the Custom Reports dialog box.

    🖈 To print a default report, display it in a Preview window and click Print.

2. Preview the custom report, and verify that it includes the desired information and is formatted properly.

3. Click Print.

4. Set the desired print options and click OK to send the print request to a printer.

ACTIVITY 3-6

Printing Custom Reports

Setup:

The My CSS Week 12.mpp file is open, the Preview window is closed, and the Custom Reports dialog box is displayed.

Scenario:

The FINISH DATES REPORT is ready for Carol, one of the project sponsors. All you need to do is to print one copy for her. Your coworker suggests that she might also appreciate seeing a copy of the custom Task Usage report provided by Project, showing progress from the beginning of the project plan through the week beginning 10/9/05.

What You Do	How You Do It
1. Print a copy of the FINISH DATES REPORT.	a. Display the FINISH DATES REPORT in the Preview window.
	b. Verify that the report has appropriate Header and Footer information, as well as all of the other desired information.
	c. Click Print.
	d. If necessary, in the Print Range box, select All.
	e. In the Copies box, if necessary, select 1 as the number of copies to be printed.
	f. Click OK.

2. Preview a copy of the custom Task Usage report, showing task progress from 8/1/05 through the week beginning 10/9/05.

   a. If necessary, **redisplay the Custom Reports dialog box.**

   b. **Select the Task Usage report.**

   c. **Click Print.**

   d. **Verify that the Print Range (All) and Copies (1) are set for the default printer.**

   e. If necessary, in the Timescale box, **select Dates and change the From date to** *8/1/05* **and the To date to** *10/9/05.*

   f. **Click Preview.**

---

3. Does the custom Task Usage report show total hours worked?

---

4. Print a copy of the Task Usage report and close the file, saving changes as needed.

   a. In the Preview window, **click Print.**

   b. **Click OK.**

   c. **Close the Reports dialog box.**

   d. **Choose File→Close.**

   e. **Click Yes** to save changes.

---

5. How might you use hard-copy printouts for your project plans?

Lesson 3 Follow-up

Well done! You have learned what it takes to customize a report. You can now create your own reports, modify their headers and footers, add pictures, modify margin settings, and print reports as needed. These skills will help you supply applicable project plan information to your project team so that they can be as successful as possible. You're now ready to reuse project plan information.

1. What benefits do you expect from creating custom reports for your own project plans?

2. What factors might influence your decision whether or not you create custom reports or use the default reports supplied by Project? Discuss your answers with the class.

LESSON 4
Reusing Project Plan Information

Lesson Objectives:

In this lesson, you will reuse existing project plan information.

You will:

* Create a template based on an existing project plan.

* Create a custom view.

* Make custom views available to other project plans using the Organizer.

* Share resources with other project plans.

* Create a master project plan using existing project plans.

Introduction

You've done an enormous amount of work on your project plan so far. You've entered data, created custom tables, and custom reports. Some of these items may be used in other projects. In this lesson, you will learn how Project can help you leverage existing project plan elements for use in other projects.

Will all of this effort you've invested in creating custom project plan elements be wasted once this project is complete? It doesn't have to be. As you use Project more and more, you may begin to see common patterns arising between your project plans. Maybe you are responsible for overseeing plans for similar products. Or maybe you work with the same people on every project. Whatever the similarities, Project can help you reuse custom elements from one project plan in others.

TOPIC A

Create a Project Plan Template

As you build more and more project plans, you may find yourself repeating certain steps in each file—creating the same custom table, for instance. You could continue to create these custom elements every time if you want, but there's an easier way. This topic will show you how to include such common elements in a new template project plan file.

Including common plan elements in a template saves everyone time and ensures consistency between plan files—especially if your plans have to meet some corporate standards. Since a template already includes project plan elements that you need to do your job, you can spend your time managing the project rather than making sure the plan includes that custom costs report. Having consistency between your plan files also makes it efficient for you to transition between one project and another—tables and reports look the same, making it easier for you to work. If each plan were vastly different, you would spend a lot of time just trying to figure out where to enter or display information. Consistent project plans make for consistent tracking and reporting methods.

Templates

Definition:

A *template* is a Project file that contains predefined project plan information. Templates are used to provide you with a starting point when you create a new project plan. Templates typically contain generic information (company names, logos, and so on) and project plan setup and formatting (margin settings, headers and footers, and so on) common to plans of its type. Although templates can contain task and resource information, too, the critical aspect of a template is that it only contains required elements to meet an agreed-upon standard, common to your company. Stuff considered to be "nice to have" or "extra" should not be included in the template file.

 Project template files have a ".mpt" file extension.

Example:

> When you perform a Complete install of Project on your computer, you also install a variety of predefined templates supplied by Project. These templates are based on common business processes, types of products, and typical events.

Global.mpt

> Sometimes called the global file, the *Global.mpt* is the generic Project template that contains default settings on which all new project plans are based. Typically, the Global.mpt file determines which view is displayed at startup, the units of work displayed (hours, days, or weeks) in a plan, and whether or not schedule calculations are performed automatically or manually. The Global.mpt template may also include custom elements deemed necessary by your company.

How to Create a Project Plan Template

Procedure Reference:

> Even with 20 existing templates provided by Project to choose from, they may not provide you with a suitable solution for your needs. In these cases, you will need to create your own template. You can create one from a blank project, but you would need to add all the items outside the context of a project plan. A better solution is to use an existing project plan that already contains all of the elements you want included in your template.

> To create a project plan template from an existing project plan:

1. Open the existing project plan that has all the necessary elements you want to include in the template.

2. Make the project plan more generic by removing any project-specific information.

3. Choose File→Save As.

4. Give the template a descriptive name.

5. From the Save As Type drop-down list, select Template (*.mpt).

6. Click Save.

7. Select data in the current project plan to be omitted from the template.

8. Click Save again.

9. Close the template.

10. Use the template to check that the template contains the anticipated content.

Custom Templates Distribution

> If you are ever asked to provide your custom templates to others, all you have to do is provide them with the appropriate template (*.mpt) file. Typically, custom templates are stored on your hard drive in the Documents And Settings*user name*\Application Data\Microsoft\Templates folder, where *user name* is the user name to log on to the computer. This is worth mentioning, because the templates that come with Project are stored in a different location on your hard drive, the Program Files\Microsoft Office\Templates\1033 folder.

Custom Template Modification

You can add and remove elements from your custom templates at any time. If you edit a custom template, note that any modifications you make will not be reflected in any project plan that may have initially used the template. Only new project plans based on the updated template will reflect the changes.

ACTIVITY 4-1

Creating a Template from an Existing Project Plan

Data Files:

- CSS Week 13.mpp

Setup:

All project plans are closed and Project is open.

Scenario:

The CSS Training Manual project plan is nearing completion and it already contains the majority of elements you would want to use again the next time you and your team members are called upon to create a training manual. To save yourself time and effort on similar projects in the future, you decide to base a new, project-generic template on the latest CSS project plan file.

What You Do	How You Do It
1. Remove any CSS project-specific information and references from the CSS Week 13 project plan.	a. Open CSS Week 13.mpp.
	b. In Task 0, **change the title from "CSS Training Manual" to** *Training Manual,* as shown in the following graphic.

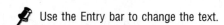
Use the Entry bar to change the text.

c. **Remove the split from Task 5.** (In the Gantt Chart, position the mouse pointer over the task bar until you see a four-headed arrow, and then drag the right half of the task back so that it reconnects with the left half of the task.)

 Zooming in on Task 5 may make it easier to remove the split.

d. For Task 7, **remove the split.**

Remove the hyperlink to the outline document. (Right-click the task's Indicators field and choose Hyperlink→Remove Hyperlink.)

From the Deliverables column, **delete the text "CSS Outlines.doc."**

e. In Task 9, although no Constraint icon is displayed in the Indicators column because the task is complete, **change the constraint type to As Soon As Possible.** (Display the Advanced tab in the task's Task Information dialog box.)

 Depending upon how you use your own project plans, you may also want to remove resources.

2. **Save the project plan as a template named *MY TRAINING MANUAL*, omitting baselines, actual values, and whether or not tasks have been published to the Microsoft Project Server. Close the new template.**

a. **Choose File→Save As.**

b. **Name the template *MY TRAINING MANUAL***

c. **From the Save As Type drop-down list, select Template (*.mpt).**

d. **Click Save.**

 If a file by that name already exists, click OK to overwrite it.

LESSON 4

e. In the Save As Template dialog box, **check the Values Of All Baselines, Actual Values, and Whether Tasks Have Been Published To Project Server options** to omit the data from the template.

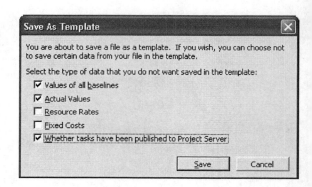

f. **Click Save.**

g. **Close the template file.**

3. **Make a new project plan based on the template you just created.**

a. **Choose File→New.**

b. In the New Project task pane, **click the On My Computer link.**

c. In the Templates dialog box, on the General tab, **select MY TRAINING MANUAL.mpt and click OK.**

4. **Explore the new project plan.**

What project plan elements are already included for you in the new plan?

5. Display the new project plan's Project Information dialog box.

    What's the start date?

___

6. Display the project plan's statistics.

    Does the new plan contain baseline or actual values?

    Save the project plan as *My New Training Manual.mpp*

Topic B

Create a Custom Combination View

You switch views in Project all the time. Sometimes, you may find yourself changing tables in a view or toggling back and forth between two views to compare plan details. Similar to how you can create custom tables to display particular columns of data together, you can also create custom views that allow you to display exactly the information you want. This topic will show you how.

Being able to quickly display custom views allows you to quickly and accurately enter and display related project plan information without having to modify a view each time. For example, if you're curious about seeing a resource's scheduled tasks and you also want to review the Resource Usage view to see what other tasks they will be working on, you could switch back and forth between the two views, but it's difficult to remember who's doing what and when. It would be much easier if you could display both views on the screen at the same time. You can, by making a custom view.

How to Create a Custom View

Procedure Reference:

Project allows you to create two kinds of custom views: single and combination. A *single view* displays one chart, sheet, or form view. A *combination view* displays two different views on the same screen, one on the top and one on the bottom. The bottom pane usually displays details about the task or resource selected in the top pane's view. Custom views can be created in an open project plan from scratch or by creating a copy of an existing default view.

To create a new custom view from scratch:

1. Choose View→More Views.

2. Click New, select either Single View or Combination View, and then click OK.

To Create a Single View

a.   Provide a descriptive name for the new single view.

b.   Select a screen type.

c.   Specify the table to be displayed.

d.   Select a task group, filter, and highlighting, if desired.

e.   Select whether or not you want the new combination view to be listed in the Views menu.

To Create a Combination View

a.   Provide a descriptive name for the new combination view.

b.   Select the view to be displayed in the top pane.

c.   Select the view to be displayed in the bottom pane.

d.   Select whether or not you want the new combination view to be listed in the Views menu.

3.   Click OK to create the custom view.

4.   Test the new custom view, if desired.

Copy Existing Views

Rather than create a new view from scratch, you can tinker with a copy of an existing view. You should first create a copy of the existing view in the More Views dialog box. Doing so preserves the original view, while creating the new view definition in the open project plan.

ACTIVITY 4-2

Creating Custom Views

Setup:

My New Training Manual.mpp is open.

Scenario:

Earlier, when you updated the task progress for the CSS Training Manual, you switched views and displayed the Tracking table. However, it wasn't readily apparent how the progress affected the project plan. To see that, you had to switch back to Tracking Gantt view. For the sake of efficiency, you want to enter data directly in the Tracking table while viewing the Tracking Gantt chart.

What You Do	How You Do It
1. Create a new single view called *MY TASK PROGRESS SHEET* using the Tracking table from Task Sheet view.	a. **Choose View→More Views.**
	b. **Click New.**
	c. If necessary, **select Single View.**
	d. **Click OK** to display the View Definition dialog box.
	e. In the Name text box, **type** *MY TASK PROGRESS SHEET*
	f. From the Screen drop-down list, **select Task Sheet.**
	g. From the Table drop-down list, **select Tracking.**
	h. From the Group drop-down list, **select No Group.**
	i. From the Filter drop-down list, **select All Tasks.**

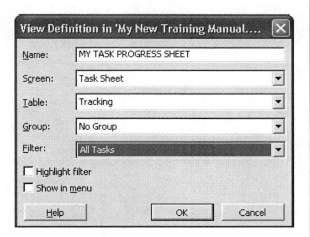

j. **Click OK** to create the new custom single view.

2. Apply the new MY TASK PROGRESS SHEET view.

    How does this single custom view help you enter task progress data?

    That makes entering task progress data easier, but you still need to make it more conve-
    nient to see the data's effect.

---

3. **Create a new view named *MY
    TRACKING VIEW* that displays both
    the Tracking Gantt view and the MY
    TASK PROGRESS SHEET view at the
    same time.**

    a. **Choose View→More Views.**

    b. **Click New.**

    c. **Select Combination View.**

    d. **Click OK** to display the View Definition
        dialog box.

    e. In the Name text box, **type *MY TRACKING
        VIEW***

    f. Under the Views Displayed heading, from
        the Top drop-down list, **select Tracking
        Gantt.**

    g. From the Bottom drop-down list, **select
        MY TASK PROGRESS SHEET.**

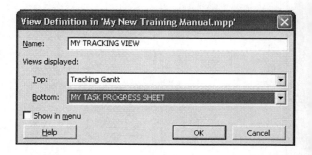

    h. **Click OK** to create the new combination
        view.

---

4. **Apply the new MY TRACKING VIEW and select a task of your choice in the top Tracking Gantt pane.** (You may need to click the Go To Selected Task button on the Standard toolbar to see the task in the Tracking Gantt chart.)

    What happens in the bottom MY TASK PROGRESS SHEET pane when you select a task?

5. **What's missing from the Tracking Gantt chart?**

TOPIC C

Make Custom Views Available to Other Project Plans

With your custom view created, does that mean you need to create it in every plan you work on? Of course not. In this topic, you will see how you can make your custom elements available to other project plans.

Being able to use custom views or other custom elements in other plans will make your life easier. You could add the view to a template, but in many cases, custom views are a matter of preference rather than a requirement. Using the same view in another plan ensures that the custom views will be identical, so information will be displayed exactly as it was in the original plan.

The Organizer

As shown in Figure 4-1, the *Organizer* is a tool for copying, deleting, and renaming project elements such as calendars, reports, tables, and views. To copy elements between any two project plan and/or template files, both the source file (the one containing the element to be copied) and the destination file (the file that will receive the element) must be opened with the file name displayed in the Available In drop-down list. The Organizer can be launched from the Tools menu, as well as from other locations where you would be likely to customize elements, like the Custom Reports, More Views, and More Tables dialog boxes.

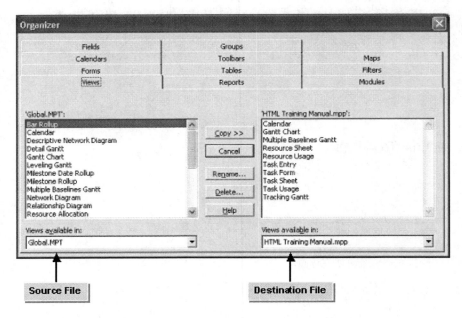

Figure 4-1: *The Organizer.*

How to Make Custom Views Available to Other Project Plans

Procedure Reference:

To make custom views available to other project plans:

1. If necessary, open the project plan that currently contains the custom view(s)—the source file project plan.

2. Open the project plan that you want to receive the custom view(s)—the destination file project plan.

3. Display the Organizer dialog box using one of the following methods:
    *   Choose View→More Views and click Organizer.
    *   Choose Tools→Organizer.

4. If necessary, select the Views tab.

5. On the left-hand side, select the source file project plan from the Views Available In drop-down list.

6. Select the custom view(s) from the source file's list of views.

7. On the right side, if necessary, select the destination file project plan from the Views Available In drop-down list.

8. Click Copy.

9. Click Close.

Copying Other Elements

You can use the previously mentioned procedure steps to copy other project plan elements, besides custom views, between open project plans. The only change would be to select the appropriate element's tab in the Organizer dialog box and then select that element. For instance, if you wanted to copy a custom table from one plan to another, you would display the Organizer dialog box, select the Tables tab, pick the custom table from the source file project plan's list, and then click Copy.

ACTIVITY 4-3

Copying Custom Views from One Plan to Another

Data Files:

- HTML Training Manual.mpp

Setup:

My New Training Manual.mpp is open with the custom combination MY TRACKING VIEW applied.

Scenario:

Your next project, the HTML Training Manual, was created using the Blank Project template, which doesn't include the custom views that you just created, MY TASK PROGRESS SHEET and MY TRACKING VIEW. Since those views will make your job easier, use the Organizer tool to copy them into the HTML Training Manual project plan.

What You Do	How You Do It
1. Copy MY TASK PROGRESS SHEET and MY TRACKING VIEW from your new training manual project plan to the HTML Training Manual file.	a. Open HTML Training Manual.mpp.
	b. Choose View→More Views. The HTML Training Manual project plan file doesn't contain the custom views yet.
	c. Click Organizer to display the Organizer dialog box.

 Because the custom combination view uses the custom single view, both views must be copied.

d. With the Views tab selected, on the left side of the Organizer dialog box from the Views Available In drop-down list, **select My New Training Manual.mpp.**

e. From the My New Training Manual.mpp views list, **drag to select both MY TASK PROGRESS SHEET and MY TRACKING VIEW.**

f. If necessary, on the right side of the Organizer dialog box, from the Views Available In drop-down list, **select HTML Training Manual.mpp.**

g. **Click Copy** to copy the two custom views to the HTML Training Manual's project plan.

h. **Close the Organizer dialog box.**

2. **Apply MY TRACKING VIEW to the HTML Training Manual project plan and display a task in the Tracking Gantt chart.**

    How will using this custom view benefit you in this project plan?

3. **What's another way to include common elements in a plan so that they are available as soon as the project plan file is created?**

    Save the HTML Training Manual as *My HTML Training Manual.mpp*

DISCOVERY ACTIVITY 4-4

Copying Other Custom Elements Between Project Plans

Scenario:

My New Training Manual.mpp contains a few other custom project plan elements that would be useful to other project plans. (See Table 4-1.) When you're done, close both project plans.

Table 4-1: *Custom Project Plan Elements in My New Training Manual.mpp*

Custom Elements	Custom Element Name
Tables	BASELINE/INTERIM DATES, FINISH DATES
Reports	FINISH DATES REPORT

1. Copy the BASELINE/INTERIM DATES and FINISH DATES tables from My New Training Manual.mpp to My HTML Training Manual.mpp.

2. Copy the FINISH DATES REPORT from My New Training Manual.mpp to My HTML Training Manual.mpp, and then save and close both project plans.

TOPIC D

Share Resources

Rarely are a plan's resources your own. It's quite common for your team members to be part of a larger pool of resources, as they may be working on project plans other than yours. This topic will show you how to share resources.

Sharing resources allows you to schedule work across projects while enabling you to track and manage resource conflicts. This prevents the resource from becoming overallocated. If you don't properly share resources, you could unknowingly wind up scheduling a person for double duty, not only burning the person out, but perhaps creating tension between yourself and other project managers who use the same resources.

Resource Pool

A *resource pool* is nothing more than a separate Project file that contains only resource information—names, rates, and so on—that you can assign to tasks in one or more project plans. (See Figure 4-2.) Each project plan that uses the resources listed in the resource pool is called a *sharer file*. Resource pools provide sharer files with a centralized, consistent, and current source of resource information, thereby helping to prevent resource overallocation. Resource pools also eliminate the need for the project managers to re-enter resource information.

When saving a new resource pool, it's a good idea to put the words "Resource Pool" or "RP" somewhere in the file name so that it can be distinguished from other project plans.

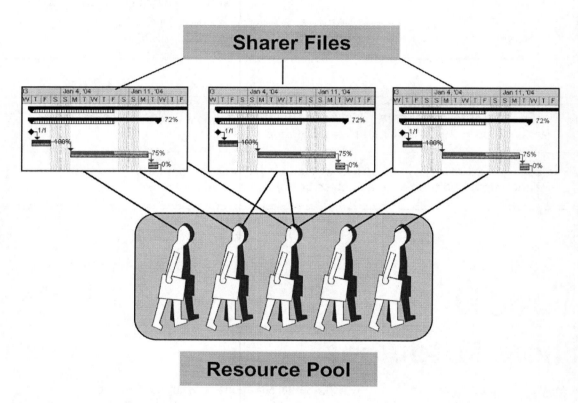

Figure 4-2: *A resource pool.*

Sharer Projects

You don't need a resource pool to share resources. You can borrow resources from other project plans. Unlike a resource pool which contains only resource information, a *sharer project* is an actual project plan—one that contains tasks, costs, assignments, and so on—that happens to contain some resources you want to use in another project plan, or sharer file. In effect, the sharer project becomes a resource pool. However, sharer projects are less common than resource pools because the ability to monitor resource allocation is limited to just the linked plans.

Enterprise Resources

All resources available to an entire organization are called *enterprise resources*. Often maintained by a personnel or human resources department, an enterprise resource pool may include all employees, contractors, materials, and vendors—any source that might be considered a resource to the company. Although an enterprise resource pool may sound like a good idea, such large pools can often be problematic to work with because of their size and potentially far-reaching effects on interrelated project plans throughout an organization.

How to Share Resources

Procedure Reference:

To share resources using an existing resource pool:

1. Open the resource pool file you want to use as read-only.

2. Verify which project plans, if any, are sharing the pool. (Choose Tools→Resource Sharing→Share Resources.)

   If the resource pool is already linked to a sharer project, you will be prompted to open the resource pool as read-only.

3. Open the project plan that will share the resources—the sharer project.

4. In the sharer project, choose Tools→Resource Sharing→Share Resources.

   You can also display the Resource Management toolbar and click the Share Resources button.

5. Select Use Resources.

6. In the From drop-down list, select the desired open resource pool file.

7. If necessary, give the resource pool precedence.

8. Click OK.

9. Assign resources to tasks in the sharer project.

10. Level the resources, if desired.

11. Save and close the sharer project.

12. Save and close the resource pool.

Open Resource Pool Options

When you open a resource pool that is being shared by other project plans, you have a few options. You can open the resource pool as read-only. Most often, you will use this option because it allows others to work on project plans linked to the pool. If you need to modify the resource pool, you should open it as read-write; this lets you directly save edits to the pool, but it prevents sharer files from updating the resource pool. Lastly, you can open the resource pool and all sharer files as a new master project file, which you will learn about shortly.

Precedence

By default, if conflicts arise between a sharer file and a resource pool, the resource pool will overwrite the resource information in the sharer file, because the resource pool has precedence over the sharer file. For instance, if a sharer file states that Editor 1 makes $20/hour and the resource pool states that Editor 1 makes $25/hour, the $20 rate in the sharer file will be overwritten by the resource pool's $25/hour rate. Ordinarily, it's preferable to give precedence to the resource pool; however, if a project plan is considered critical, the sharer file may be given precedence.

Discontinue Sharing Resources

If the time comes when you want to stop sharing resources with a resource pool or sharer project, you can do so by selecting the Use Own Resources option in the Share Resources dialog box. When you disconnect from a resource pool, the sharer file retains assignment and resource information.

ACTIVITY 4-5

Sharing Resources Using a Resource Pool

Data Files:

- TM Resource Pool.mpp

- XML Training Manual.mpp

Setup:

All project plans are closed.

Scenario:

You have a project that needs to have resources assigned to tasks; however, you don't have a team of your own. You need to share the resources of another project plan so you can assign the tasks shown in Table 4-2.

Table 4-2: *Task Assignments for XML Training Manual*

Task	Resource
1 Start Book	Project Manager 2
3 Interview Subject Matter Expert	Project Manager 2, Subject Matter Expert 2
4 Investigate XML	Writer 1

What You Do	How You Do It
1. Display the Share Resources dialog box for the TM Resource Pool.	a. Open the resource pool TM Resource Pool.mpp.
	b. If necessary, **select the first option, Open Resource Pool Read-Only Allowing Others To Work On Projects Connected To The Pool.**
	c. **Click OK.**
	d. **Choose Tools→Resource Sharing→Share Resources.**

2. What project plans are currently sharing the resource pool?

Click Cancel to close the Share Resources dialog box.

3. **Open the XML Training Manual project plan.** This will be the sharer project.

Are there any resources in the plan's Resource Sheet?

4. **Share the resources in the TM Resource Pool with the XML Training Manual.**

    a. From the XML Training Manual project plan, **choose Tools→Resource Sharing→ Share Resources** to display the Share Resources dialog box.

    b. **Select Use Resources.**

    c. If necessary, from the From drop-down list, **select TM Resource Pool.mpp**.

    d. If necessary, **select Pool Takes Precedence.**

    e. **Click OK** to make the resource pool resources available within the XML Training Manual project plan.

5. **Assign and level the resources for the XML Training Manual project plan.**

    Before assigning each task, you may want to position the Divide bar so the Start, Finish, and Resource Names columns are all visible. Pay particular attention to the start and finish dates for each task before and after you assign the resource.

    a. **Switch to Gantt Chart view.**

    b. In the Resource Names column, for Task 1, **assign Project Manager 2.**

    c. For Task 3, **assign Project Manager 2 and Subject Matter Expert 2.**

    d. For Task 4, **assign Writer 1.**

    e. **Choose Tools→Level Resources.**

    f. **Click Level Now.**

6. When you assigned Writer 1 to Task 4 and leveled the resources, what happened to the task's Start and Finish dates?

What happened to the critical path in the Gantt Chart?

Use Edit→Undo and Edit→Redo to toggle the task assignment to more easily see the effect of assigning Writer 1 to Task 4.

7. Display the Resource Usage view and display Writer 1.

What caused these changes when Writer 1 was assigned to Task 4?

Click the Go To Selected Task button to display tasks assigned to Writer 1.

8. What other steps might you take to resolve resource conflicts?

9. **Reassign Task 4 to Writer 2 and, if necessary, level the resources again. Close the XML sharer file, saving changes as** *My XML Training Manual.mpp*.

a. In the Resource Names column of Gantt Chart view, **reassign Task 4 to Writer 2.** This should resolve the resource conflict, because Writer 2 is available.

b. **Level the resources again.**

c. **Save the XML project plan as** *My XML Training Manual.mpp*

d. **Click OK** to update the resource pool to reflect changes for all open sharer projects.

e. **Close My XML Training Manual.mpp,** saving changes if prompted.

10. In the TM Resource Pool, **display the Share Resources dialog box.**

Identify the sharer files.

Close the Share Resources dialog box and close the resource pool.

TOPIC E

Create a Master Project Plan

Managing one project plan can be challenging by itself, but monitoring multiple project plans can be daunting. Don't worry, though; it's not as hard as you might think. In this topic, you will see how to combine several plans into one master project plan.

Putting related projects under one roof gives you the ability to work conveniently with these projects as if they were one large, consolidated project plan. You could allocate resources, apply filters, and analyze costs separately for each project and then try to reconcile any problems in each file. It's much more convenient, however, to combine them in a master plan and do these procedures once. You will likely make fewer errors and you will instantly see how one change will impact the related plans.

Master Projects

Definition:

A *master project* is a project file that contains other inserted projects. Each project inserted in the master project is called a *subproject*. Master projects are typically used as a way to consolidate smaller, related projects or phases into one plan so that they can be viewed, updated, and monitored more easily.

 When saving a master project, you will be given the option to save any changes made to subprojects.

Example:

Think of a master plan file as an administrative and organizational container. For instance, rather than running a Project Summary report on several related project plans and then trying to analyze multiple reports, you can create a master project containing those plans. Once the subprojects have been inserted into a master project, you can run one report that includes details from all of the subprojects. Using the master project in this way can provide you with all the necessary information in one report.

How to Create a Master Project Plan

Procedure Reference:

To create a master project plan:

1. Open the file that will become the master project plan.

2. In Gantt Chart view, select the row below the task where you want to insert the subproject.

3. Choose Insert→Project.

4. Locate the desired project plan file.

5. Click Insert to insert the project plan and its tasks.

6. Indent the subproject, so the master project plan becomes a summary task including the newly inserted subproject.

7. Display the subproject to ensure that all the tasks were inserted.

8. Repeat the above steps, as needed.

Project Field

One of the difficulties in working within a master project is being able to identify which tasks belong to which subprojects. There is, however, an easy way to fix that in the Entry table of Gantt Chart view. Just insert the Project field as a column next to the Task Name column, and the subproject's name will be placed right next to the task itself for easy identification.

Break a Link

At some point, you may not want the subprojects to be affected by changes in the master project. You can break the link between the subproject and its source file by selecting the subproject's summary task and displaying its Task Information dialog box. On the Advanced tab, uncheck the Link To Project option to unlink the two.

ACTIVITY 4-6

Creating a Quarterly Training Manual Master Project Plan

Data Files:

- Q4 Master.mpp
- Subproject CSS.mpp
- Subproject HTML.mpp
- Subproject Unix.mpp
- Subproject XML.mpp

Setup:

All project plan files and resource pools are closed.

Scenario:

It's October 17, 2005, and the fourth quarter of Coleman Publishing's fiscal year is in full swing. You're busier than ever, and you have one project plan already in progress, and three new ones starting very shortly. You need to find an efficient way to monitor all of these plans so nothing slips through the cracks.

What You Do	How You Do It
1. Insert the CSS subproject into the Q4 Master project plan.	a. **Open Q4 Master.mpp.**
	b. In Gantt Chart view, below the project summary task, **select the Task Name field in the second row.** This is where the subproject will be inserted.

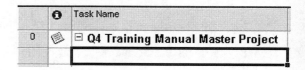

	❶	Task Name
0	📝	⊟ **Q4 Training Manual Master Project**

	c. **Choose Insert→Project.**
	d. From the My Documents folder, **select Subproject CSS.mpp.**
	e. **Click Insert.**

2. In Gantt Chart view, what do you notice about the master project and the inserted subproject?

_____

3. **Display the task information for Task 1.** (Double-click the CSS Training Manual task name.)

   What's the name of the displayed dialog box and what information does it include?

   Close the dialog box.

_____

4. **Show the tasks for the CSS Training Manual subproject and display Task 21 in the Gantt Chart.**

   Why hasn't this task been marked complete?

_____

5. **Hide the tasks for the CSS Training Manual subproject and insert the remaining subprojects (HTML, Unix, and XML).**

   a. **Click the minus sign (-) to hide the CSS Training Manual subproject's tasks.**

   b. **Select the Task Name field below CSS Training Manual.**

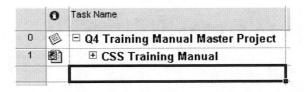

   c. **Display the Insert Project dialog box.**

d. **Select Subproject HTML.mpp, press and hold down Shift, and select Subproject XML.mpp** to select the range of all three files.

Subproject CSS.mpp
Subproject HTML.mpp
Subproject Unix.mpp
Subproject XML.mpp
TM Resource Pool.mpp

e. **Click Insert.**

6. **What are the starting dates for the three newly inserted subprojects?**

7. **Display all tasks in all subprojects and view the Project Summary Report.**

What's the scheduled duration for the master project plan? _____

How many days remain in the master project plan? _____

What's the percentage complete for the master project plan? _____

Close the Preview window and the Reports dialog box.

Save the master project as *My Q4 Master.mpp*, **saving changes to all the subprojects. Close the master project.**

Lesson 4 Follow-up

In this lesson, you have learned what it takes to reuse existing project plan information to make your job easier. You created your own project plan template, providing a starting point for your next plan. You made your own custom combination view to see project plan data just the way you want. Then, you used the Organizer to copy the custom view to another project plan. On a larger scale, you used an existing resource pool to share resources between project plans. You also took related project plans and created one large master project plan out of it. All of these skills combined will help you develop your project plans faster and more efficiently. You're now ready to begin collaborating with others on a project plan.

1. **What benefits do you expect to gain from reusing project plan elements? What elements might you reuse?**

2. Is your company likely to use resource pools to help monitor resource usage? If so, why? If not, why not?

Follow-up

In this course, you have successfully exchanged project plan data with other applications, updated project plans, created custom reports, and reused project plan information. With all of these worthy skills, you can now communicate more effectively with stakeholders and team members as you monitor, correct, and report on a project plan throughout its life cycle.

1. **Keeping your current project management methods in mind, how might you use Project to help you with project plans going forward? Will you keep your old methods or will you move to a Project-centered approach to project management? Or will you mix the old methods with some of Project's features? Discuss your response with the class.**

2. **What is the single feature of Project that you will certainly use? Which features will you least likely use?**

3. **Back at work, what role will you most likely have in future project plans? How can you see your department or company using Project?**

What's Next?

Microsoft Project 2003: Level 2 is the last in this series.

LESSON LABS

Due to classroom setup constraints, some labs cannot be keyed in sequence immediately following their associated lesson. Your instructor will tell you whether your labs can be practiced immediately following the lesson or whether they require separate setup from the main lesson content.

LESSON 1 LAB 1

Exporting Project Plan Information to a Web Page

Data Files:

- Periodicals Phase 1 Draft.mpp

- phase1draft-solution.html

- phase1draft-solution.gif

Setup:

This activity can be completed immediately following Lesson 1, or after students have finished the entire course. No project plans are open.

Scenario:

You've finished a project plan draft (Periodicals Phase 1 Draft.mpp) for the first stage of Coleman Publishing's new division, Coleman Publishing Periodicals. Upper management wants to review the Gantt Chart, and task, resource, and assignment details before you finalize them. Rather than distribute sections of the plan in different file formats and take the chance of leaving out some critical detail, you opt to create a Web page.

The file phase1draft-solution.html (with phase1draft-solution.gif) shows a completed example of this activity. You can compare your results to the file. This example presents one of many possible solutions, so your solution might not match exactly.

1. **Copy a picture of the Periodicals Phase 1 Draft project plan's Gantt Chart view. Save the copied picture to your My Documents folder as a GIF image file named *phase1draft.gif* from 8/1/05 to 9/18/05. (See Topic 1D for assistance.)**

2. Using the existing HTML export template, **export the Periodical Phase 1 Draft project plan as a Web page named *phase1draft.html* so that tasks, resources, assignments, and the phase1draft.gif image are all included in the HTML page.** (See Topic 1E for assistance.)

3. **Open phase1draft.html in your browser.** The picture should be displayed above the tasks, resources, and assignments.

4. **Close the browser and the Periodicals Phase 1 Draft.mpp project plan in Project without saving any changes.**

LESSON 2 LAB 1

Updating a Project Plan

Data Files:

- Update Phase 1.mpp

- Update Phase 1-solution.mpp

Setup:

This activity can be completed immediately following Lesson 2, or after students have finished the entire course.

Scenario:

It's August 8, 2005, and phase 1 of the Coleman Publishing Periodicals plan, Update Phase 1.mpp, has been underway for a week now. It's time for you to begin tracking task progress to keep the project plan information current. You've just finished talking to the Manager and Business Advisor about the status of their tasks. The Manager reports that Task 3 is done and it actually lasted just a day, so you will need to update the duration. For Task 4, the Business Advisor actually worked 8 hours Tuesday, but was out sick Wednesday. He just called and said he will be back to work Wednesday, 8/10. Reschedule the uncompleted work for the entire project to begin then. Then save an interim plan to record the new dates.

Update Phase 1-solution.mpp shows a completed example of this activity. You can compare your results to this file. This file presents one of many possible solutions, so your solution might not match exactly.

1. **Change the current date of the Update Phase 1 project plan to *8/8/05*.** (See Topic 2A for assistance.)

2. In the Tracking table, for Task 3, **update % Complete as 100 percent and reduce the Actual Duration to 1 day.** (See Topic 2A for assistance.)

3. For Task 4, **update the actual hours worked to 8 hours,** reflecting the Business Advisor's work. (See Topic 2A for assistance.)

4. **Reschedule uncompleted work for the Project to start after 8/9/05.** (See Topic 2D for assistance.)

5. **Save an interim baseline for the entire project plan.** (See Topic 2G for assistance.)

6. **Display the project plan's statistics.** (See Topic 2G for assistance.)

   In days, what is the variance between the project plan's baseline and current finish dates?

7. **Save the project plan as *My Update Phase 1.mpp* and close it.**

LESSON 3 LAB 1

Creating a Custom Report that Shows Remaining Critical Tasks

Data Files:
- Phase 1 Custom Report.mpp
- Phase 1 Custom Report-solution.mpp

Setup:
This activity can be completed immediately following Lesson 3 or after students have finished the entire course.

Scenario:
It's September 6, 2005, and there's only a week left in Phase 1 of the Coleman Periodicals plan. Your boss wants to see a hard copy list of just the critical tasks that remain on the schedule so she can identify those tasks that may require additional resources or time should they slip. A couple of things to keep in mind: your boss is very busy, so a one-page report would work best for her, and her desk looks like a tornado hit it, so you may want to customize the header and footer information to make the report easily identifiable.

 You can compare your results to this file, Phase 1 Custom Report-solution.mpp. It contains a report that shows a completed example for this activity. This file presents one of many possible solutions, so your solution might not match exactly.

1. Set the Phase 1 Custom Report project plan's current date to *9/6/05*.

2. Create a new task-based report named *REMAINING CRITICAL TASKS*. The report should filter the entire project's Schedule table so that only Critical tasks are shown.

3. Customize the report so either the header or footer information at least includes the report title, the project's current date, and your boss' name is displayed. Add and format any other information as you see fit.

4. Modify the report's margins so all the columns of information fit on one page.

5. Print one copy of the REMAINING CRITICAL TASKS report.

🖈 If you don't have access to a printer, just view it in a Preview window.

6. Save the project plan as *My Phase 1 Custom Report.mpp* and close it.

LESSON 4 LAB 1

Creating a Master Project Plan with Shared Elements

Data Files:

- New Business Master.mpp
- Periodicals Master.mpp
- Periodicals Phase 1.mpp
- Periodicals Phase 2.mpp
- Periodicals Phase 3.mpp
- Periodicals Phase 4.mpp
- Periodicals Master-solution.mpp

Setup:

This activity can be completed immediately following Lesson 4, or after students have finished the entire course. The New Business Master project plan file already contains some custom project plan elements that you can use to better track subproject tasks.

Scenario:

With Phase 1 of the Coleman Periodicals new business plan coming to an end, and with three phases remaining, you need a fast and efficient way to monitor and report on tasks in all four phases of the overall project plan.

The Periodicals Master-solution.mpp is a completed file of this activity. You can compare your results to this file.

1. From the New Business Master project plan, **copy the SUBPROJECT INFO view, the SUBPROJECT TASK LIST table, and the SUBPROJECT DETAILS report to the Periodicals Master.** (See Topic 4C for assistance.)

2. **Add the four periodical phases as subprojects to the Periodicals Master project.** (See Topic 4E for assistance.)

 There are no links between subprojects in this master project plan. However, because these phases are sequential, you may want to link the last task in each subproject phase to the first actual task in the succeeding phase.

3. In the Periodicals Master, **create and apply a new combination view named** *GANTT/SUBPROJECT DETAIL* **that shows the Gantt Chart view on the top and the SUBPROJECT INFO on the bottom.** This will make it easier to identify which tasks belong to which subproject. (See Topic 4B for assistance.)

4. **Display all subproject tasks and print the SUBPROJECT DETAILS report** to see completed tasks and the remaining master project schedule.

   ⚠ If the subproject tasks aren't expanded, the report will not print.

 If you don't have access to a printer, you can preview the report instead.

5. **Save the master project as *My Periodicals Master.mpp* and save changes to all subprojects. Close any remaining open project plans.**

NOTES

SOLUTIONS

Lesson 1

Activity 1-1

3. **In Gantt Chart view of the new project plan, where did Project import the contents that were in Excel's Name column?**

    In the new project plan's Task Name column.

4. **Where did Project import the contents that were in Excel's Notes column?**

    In the new project plan's Indicators column.

5. **Notice the Indicators column. What did Project place on each task?**

    Project automatically placed a Start No Earlier Than constraint on each task.

6. **Based on your knowledge of what is generally required in a project plan, what elements still need to be entered and/or completed before you begin using this new plan?**

    Answers will vary, but may include: adding general project information, assigning resources, linking and modifying tasks, setting calendars, entering resources, determining and setting durations, starts and finishes, and so on.

Activity 1-2

4. **Are any database fields already mapped to Project fields?**

    Yes. The Notes field is already mapped because Project recognized the database field name and found a matching field name in the Project field list.

6. **From the database, where did Project import the Resource Name and Notes fields?**

    In My CSS Project Plan's Resource Name and Indicators columns, respectively, in the plan's Resource Sheet.

7. **Were any unwanted database fields imported? For instance, was data from the database's Department, First Name, Last Name, or Title fields added to the plan's Resource Sheet?**

    No, not if the previous steps were done properly. However, Project itself automatically populated many of the other columns with default values, such as max values.

Activity 1-3

2. **What's the estimated total cost for the CSS Book project?**

    $16,809.30.

Activity 1-4

4. **In the Word document, can you edit any of the task names?**

No. The Copy Picture tool creates a graphic image. So, once the picture has been pasted, any text or data in the picture cannot be edited.

Activity 1-5

4. **What exported project plan information is displayed in the Web page?**

Answers may include: The project plan title, project start and finish dates, and all task, resource, and assignment information.

Lesson 2

Activity 2-1

3. **When you pressed Enter, what fields were filled in?**

Because Task 1 is a milestone, which has no duration or cost associated with it, only the Actual Start and Actual Finish fields were filled in with 8/1/05.

5. **When you changed the Actual Duration to 1 day, what fields were affected?**

For Task 3, the Actual Finish date changed from 8/2/05 to 8/1/05 and the actual costs were cut in half. Several fields were also updated in both the Research Phase summary task and the CSS Training Manual project summary task, reflecting Task 3's progress.

6. **When you changed the Actual Work hours to 32 hours, what fields were affected?**

For Task 4, the Actual Start and Actual Finish dates were added, % Complete changed to 100%, Remaining Duration changed to 0 days, Actual Duration changed to 4 days, and Actual Cost was recorded. Again, several fields were also updated in both the Research Phase summary task and the CSS Training Manual project summary task, reflecting the addition of Task 4's progress.

Activity 2-2

1. **What do you notice about tasks 1, 3, and 4 now that their progress has been updated?**

Answers will vary, but may include: tasks 1, 3, and 4 have check marks in their Indicators columns to denote completion. Tasks 3 and 4 have black progress bars displayed inside their respective task bars. Tasks 3 and 4 are 100 percent complete. The duration of Task 3 has been cut in half, so Task 4 begins a day earlier.

Notice the current finish date. For Task 3, after you reduced the duration from 2 days to 1, did the finish date change from the original 10/19?

No. When you reduced the duration of Task 3 by one day, you might have thought the finish date would have moved in 1 day. But the finish date remains at 10/19 because Task 9 has a Start No Earlier Than restraint on it. Since the 1-day change was prior to Task 9, the finish date remains unaffected.

2. According to the Project Summary bar, how much progress has been made?

9%.

According to the Research Phase Summary bar, how much progress has been made?

71%.

4. Is the Research Phase ahead or behind schedule?

Because the progress line peaks to the right of the status date, the Research Phase appears to be a couple of days ahead of schedule. However, because the chart displays a weekend, it can be deceiving.

5. What's the current Finish Variance for Task 2, the Research Phase summary task?

At this point, the Research Phase is -1, 1 day ahead. Because Task 3 only took 1 day instead of 2, tasks 4 and 5 were able to start earlier.

Activity 2-3

3. Do you have to increase or decrease the split between the sections to account for the 1-day interruption?

No. By default, Project inserts a 1-day interruption when you split a task.

4. Now what's the Finish Variance for Task 2, the Research Phase summary task?

At this point, the Research Phase's Finish Variance is "0." Because Task 5 took one more day than expected, the project plan lost the day it had gained.

Activity 2-4

3. What happened when you rescheduled the uncompleted work?

Task 7 was added to the project plan's critical path.

4. What happened to the project plan's finish date?

It was pushed out to 10/20.

Activity 2-5

2. How many of the remaining tasks have slipped as a result of rescheduling Task 7?

All of them.

3. Besides applying a filter, such as Slipping Tasks, what other ways could you use Project to check to see what tasks are behind schedule?

Answers will vary, but may include: display the Variance table, Tracking Gantt view, and/or progress lines.

Activity 2-6

2. Which of the remaining tasks are on the critical path?

All of the remaining tasks are on the critical path.

Activity 2-7

1. **How far has the Finish date slipped?**

   Despite the fact that it looks like the Finish date has slipped an entire day in Gantt Chart view, it has only slipped 0.25 days.

Activity 2-8

4. **Using the CSS Training Manual project summary task, Task 0, what's the difference between the project's Baseline Finish date and the Interim Finish 1 date?**

   The Interim Finish 1 date is 1 day later.

5. **Comparing the Baseline Finish date and the Interim Finish 1 date for task summaries, during which phase did the plan slip?**

   The Outline Phase. This is the first summary task where the Interim Finish 1 date is later than the Baseline Finish date, showing the project plan slipped from the baseline plan at some point during that phase.

Activity 2-10

2. **What do you notice about Task 7?**

   Answers will vary, but may include: The Indicators column shows a hyperlink icon and the ScreenTip displays the file name. Task text remains normal—no text is blue and under-lined, as is typical of applying a hyperlink.

4. **How might you use hyperlinks in your projects?**

   Answers will vary, but may include: to provide links to resources on the Web; to connect applicable documents to a project plan or task; and to provide access to job aids or other reference materials.

Lesson 2 Follow-up

Lesson 2 Lab 1

6. **In days, what is the variance between the project plan's baseline and current finish dates?**

   4 working days.

Lesson 3

Activity 3-1

1. **What columns of information are displayed?**

   The table shows columns for ID, Task Name, Actual Finish, Baseline Finish, Interim 1 Finish, and Finish Variance fields.

4. **Are all the columns of information displayed on the first page of the report?**

   No. The left page shows columns for ID, Task Name, Actual Finish, Baseline Finish, and Interim 1 Finish. The right page contains the Finish Variance column.

5. **What other information is displayed at the top and bottom of the report pages?**

   Answers will vary, but may include: the report name, the date, the project title, and the manager's name are shown at the top of the report pages; and the page number is shown at the bottom of the report pages.

Activity 3-2

3. **Does the header and footer information you entered look like you expected it to? If not, discuss your expectations with the class. How might you change the information to be displayed as you want it?**

   Answers will vary, but may include: place the information in the Left alignment or Right alignment tabs; or format the text font attributes.

   What other information might you include in the Header and Footer areas? Discuss your ideas with the class.

   Answers will vary, but may include: the current time; personal notes you may want to include on each page; file names; total number of pages; cost information; and so on.

   Is the Finish Variance column still on the second page of the report?

   Yes. Headers and footers have no effect on how information is displayed horizontally on a page.

Activity 3-3

2. **Which preview do you find more useful? The Page Setup dialog box's Preview area or the Preview window? Why?**

   Answers will vary, but may include: The Page Setup dialog box's Preview area provides convenience because you can see the header and footer formatting results immediately; you can resize an image and format text as needed. The Preview window shows you the "big picture," and allows you to see both header and footer elements on screen at the same time and in the context of the report.

Activity 3-4

2. **Is the Finish Variance column now on the report's first page?**

   Yes.

What other methods might you try to get more information on a printed page?

Answers will vary, but may include: increase paper size; modify top and bottom margins; decrease font sizes; and so on.

Activity 3-5

3. What happened to the report information after you increased the top margin?

All of the header and report content moved down to accommodate the larger top margin. The footer information was unaffected by the change.

Activity 3-6

3. Does the custom Task Usage report show total hours worked?

Yes, for each task (last column), as well as for the entire project plan (last row on page 2).

5. How might you use hard-copy printouts for your project plans?

Answers will vary, but may include: for storing backup copies of a project plan; to take a snapshot of a project plan; to distribute at meetings; as training materials; and so on.

Lesson 4

Activity 4-1

4. What project plan elements are already included for you in the new plan?

Answers will vary, but may include: notes; constraints; a task list displaying outline numbers; the custom Deliverables column; custom tables and reports; durations; resource names; rates; project properties; project plan information; and others.

5. What's the start date?

The project's start date is the same as the project plan that was used to create the template, 8/1/05. This will need to be changed each time a new project plan is created using this template.

6. Does the new plan contain baseline or actual values?

No. These values were omitted when the template was created. However, because resource rates are included, Current Cost and Remaining Cost values are present.

Activity 4-2

2. **How does this single custom view help you enter task progress data?**

Rather than requiring two actions, changing the view to Task Sheet and displaying the Tracking table, before you can enter task progress data, your new custom view displays the Tracking table in Task Sheet view by default. So all you have to do is switch to your custom view and start entering task progress information, such as actual and percent-complete data, without having to switch tables first.

4. **What happens in the bottom MY TASK PROGRESS SHEET pane when you select a task?**

The selected task's tracking information is displayed at the same time, so you can easily enter each task's progress data while seeing the task displayed in the Tracking Gantt chart.

5. **What's missing from the Tracking Gantt chart?**

Baseline bars. Because the baseline information was removed when the template was created, the new project plan that was created using the template doesn't include a baseline.

Activity 4-3

2. **How will using this custom view benefit you in this project plan?**

The benefits of using the custom view in this project plan are the same as using it in any other plan—convenience when entering task progress data. The added benefit in this project plan is that you didn't have to take the extra time to re-create the custom views.

3. **What's another way to include common elements in a plan so that they are available as soon as the project plan file is created?**

Include all common project plan elements in a template.

Activity 4-5

2. **What project plans are currently sharing the resource pool?**

The Unix Training Manual.mpp file is sharing the TM Resource Pool.mpp.

3. **Are there any resources in the plan's Resource Sheet?**

No. You need to share the resource pool's resources.

6. **When you assigned Writer 1 to Task 4 and leveled the resources, what happened to the task's Start and Finish dates?**

Task 4's Start date remained the same and its Finish date moved from Friday 11/4/05 to Thursday 11/10/05.

What happened to the critical path in the Gantt Chart?

All tasks were moved to the critical path.

7. **What caused these changes when Writer 1 was assigned to Task 4?**

Writer 1 is already assigned to a task in the Unix Training Manual for that time frame. Because the resource pool has precedence, when resources were leveled in the XML Training Manual, Project reschedules Task 4 to start on Writer 1's first available date to avoid overallocating the resource.

8. **What other steps might you take to resolve resource conflicts?**

Answers will vary, but may include: start the less-important project later; hire more staff; change the resource; negotiate resource assignment with the other project managers; and so on.

10. **Identify the sharer files.**

Unix Training Manual.mpp and My XML Training Manual.mpp.

Activity 4-6

2. **In Gantt Chart view, what do you notice about the master project and the inserted subproject?**

Answers will vary, but may include: the Start date for the master project is now the same as its subproject; the CSS Training Manual is inserted as Task 1; the Indicators column shows a Microsoft Project icon to identify it as a project plan; CSS Training Manual tasks are rolled up; the duration for the master project's project summary task now includes the duration of the subproject; and in the Gantt Chart, the summary bars are of equal length.

3. **What's the name of the displayed dialog box and what information does it include?**

The dialog box is named Inserted Project Information, rather than Task Information. Here, you can view the subproject's name, as well as the source file location (on the Advanced tab).

4. **Why hasn't this task been marked complete?**

Because the CSS subproject plan is still in progress. Adding a subproject to a master project has no immediate impact on the subproject tasks.

6. **What are the starting dates for the three newly inserted subprojects?**

All three subprojects start on 10/31/05.

7. **What's the scheduled duration for the master project plan?** *128.75 days*.

How many days remain in the master project plan? *98.55 days*.

What's the percentage complete for the master project plan? *23%*.

GLOSSARY

AutoFilter
A method of filtering a column of data in a sheet view.

Check Progress pane
Part of the Project Guide, the Check Progress pane lets you quickly identify whether or not a task is on schedule or not.

combination view
A view in Project that displays two different views on the same screen, one on the top and one on the bottom. The bottom pane usually displays details about the task or resource selected in the top pane's view.

custom map
A set of instructions that you create to instruct Project as to what type of data is being imported or exported (task, resource, and assignment-related data), as well as where the data will be imported or exported.

destination file
The location where imported data will be inserted.

enterprise resources
All resources available to an entire organization.

export
Copy data out of a project plan and store it as a different file format, such as Excel workbooks, Access databases, or tab-delimited text files.

field
A location in a chart, form, or sheet that contains a unique type of information relating to an assignment, resource, or task.

filter
A set of selection criteria that allows you to include (or exclude) specific data in a view.

footer
Information printed in the bottom margin of each printed view or report page.

GIF
(Graphics Interchange Format) A common file format for graphic images used in Web pages.

Global.mpt
The generic Project template that contains default settings on which all new project plans are based.

graphics area
Any place in Project where a graphic element can be inserted, like notes, legends, and Gantt Charts.

header
Information printed in the top margin of each printed view or report page.

HTML
(HyperText Markup Language) The primary markup language for creating Web pages.

hyperlink
Text that contains an interactive link that, when clicked, displays a location in a project plan, a file in its own application, or a Web page in a browser.

import
Open task, resource, or assignment data from other file formats into new or existing project plans.

GLOSSARY

interim plan
A saved set of current start and finish dates for tasks after a plan has begun.

map
A set of instructions that instruct Project what type of data is being imported or exported (task, resource, and assignment-related data), as well as where the data will be imported or exported.

master project
A project file that contains other inserted projects. Sometimes called a consolidated project.

Organizer
A tool for copying, deleting, and renaming project elements such as calendars, reports, tables, and views.

progress bar
A thick black line displayed inside the task bar that shows how much of a task has been actually completed.

progress line
A line drawn by Project in Gantt Chart view that connects in-progress task bars. If a progress line peaks to the left, a task is behind schedule. If the progress line peaks to the right, the task is ahead of schedule.

resource pool
A separate Project file that contains only resource information—names, rates, and so on—that can be assigned to tasks in one or more project plans.

sharer file
A project plan that uses the resources listed in the resource pool.

sharer project
An actual project plan that happens to contain some resources you want to use in another project plan, or sharer file. In effect, the sharer project becomes a resource pool.

single view
A view in Project that displays one chart, sheet, or form view at a time.

source file
The location containing data that will be imported.

split task
A task with a schedule that is interrupted for a period of time.

status date
A date that you can specify to enter or view progress as of an earlier date you determine.

subproject
A project inserted in a master project.

template
A Project file that contains predefined project plan information.

Tracking Gantt chart
A chart that displays two sets of task bars—one for scheduled start and finish dates and one for baseline start and finish dates.

Variance table
A table that displays the number of days tasks are ahead or behind schedule when comparing actual dates to a project plan's baseline dates.

INDEX

A
AutoFilters, 40

C
Check Progress pane, 30
combination view, 83
Copy Picture button
  defining, 16
Copy Picture tool
  copying a picture and pasting into a Word
    document, 16
  using the options, 16
custom columns, 49
  Also See: custom fields
custom fields, 49
  Also See: custom columns
custom maps
  creating, 8
  defining, 7
custom reports
  adding a picture, 67
  creating, 58
  modifying, 63
  modifying a margin, 70
  modifying a picture, 68
  printing, 74
custom tables
  creating, 45
  editing, 46
custom templates
  distributing, 79
  editing, 80
custom views
  making available to a project plan, 88

D
destination files, 2

E
enterprise resources, 93
export, 12
Export Wizard, 12

F
fields, 6
filters
  defining, 39
  removing, 41
footers
  adding a picture, 67
  defining, 62
  modifying, 63
Format Text Font button, 63

G
General fields, 62
GIF, 16
Global.mpt, 79
graphics areas, 67
Graphics Interchange Format
  See: GIF

H
headers
  adding a picture, 67
  defining, 62
  modifying, 63
HTML, 21
hyperlinks
  defining, 53
  inserting, 53
  modifying, 53
HyperText Markup Language
  See: HTML

I
import, 2, 3, 8

INDEX

Looking for media files?

They are now conveniently located at www.elementk.com/courseware-file-downloads

Downloading is quick and easy:

1. Visit www.elementk.com/courseware-file-downloads
2. In the search field, type in either the part number or the title
3. Of the courseware titles displayed, choose your title by clicking on the name
4. Links to the data files are located in the middle of the screen
5. Follow the instructions on the screen based upon your web browser

Note that there may be other files available for download in addition to the course files.

Approximate download times:

The amount of time it takes to download your data files will vary according to the file's size and your Internet connection speed. A broadband connection is highly recommended. The average time to download a 10 mb file on a broadband connection is less than 1 minute.